Praise for *Eve, V*

Dr. Nicole Davis is spot on as a trailblazer who is giving understanding to the importance of women's role in the church. Dr. Davis's goal is to clear paths within the church for women to move from the pews to new pulpits of leadership without the resistance of a male-dominated institution. The absence of Eve in leadership within the church must be recognized if we are to move forward in building stronger churches, homes, and communities in these present dark times.

Dr. Lonise P. Bias
President, Bspeaks LLC

Eve, Where Are You? is Nicole Davis's coming-out party. And she does so with grace, a deep desire to be faithful, and a feminine warrior spirit that she discovers she has had all along and no longer has to tamp down. This book is an opportunity for every Christian woman to take a personal journey of discovery to unleash her own warrior spirit.

Louise Phipps Senft
Author, Amazon best seller, *Being Relational: The Seven
Ways to Quality Interaction & Lasting Change*

I applaud Dr. Davis for her transparency and for thoughtfully addressing this often-controversial subject. Her passion to see women fulfill their God-given purpose is evident throughout the book. I pray that all of the Eves and the Eves-to-be will be encouraged by this book designed to empower women to rise up and lead using every good and perfect gift that the Lord has deposited inside of them. And as Dr. Davis points out, there are many!

Rev. Dr. Frances "Toni" Draper
Senior pastor, Freedom Temple AME Zion Church

Nicole eloquently shares her accomplished, mountain-climbing story—illuminating the hidden treasures of women who are called by God to church leadership. Although controversial, Nicole courageously shares barrier-breaking principles in God's word—paving the way for women to take their rightful place for kingdom building. It is relatable and relevant to any woman who has been a church leader pioneer while calling out and empowering all women to be themselves! Speaking the truth in love, this book effectively challenges church organisms to rise up, embrace the heart of God, and witness the enormous impact of His church—when we equalize men and women of common mission in unconventional ways!

Niecy Dennis White
Lead pastor, The Lord's Church of Pittsburgh, PA,
Founder, Workforce Development Global Alliance (WDGA)

I met Dr. Nicole L. Davis in September of the 1981–82 school year. She was entering the sixth grade as my student. Presently, I support Dr. Davis in her post-doctoral dissertation goals for women in the structured church. Yes, secular institutions are included. Dr. Davis is Creator-God driven for women for equal chance placement, election, and advancement. I endorse this servant.

John T. Deadwyler, MS
Educator (1965–2000), Akron Public Schools; University of Akron,
Developmental Mathematics, The Ohio State University Young
Scholars Program for Calculus, Physics, and Chemistry

First and foremost, I know Nicole to be a stellar mother and teacher. She leads by example and is the perfect person to accept this mantle. The insight and wisdom that are shared in this book are exactly what women need to read and understand specially about their position in leadership as women. This book holds powerful keys to unlock the awareness that many women need to know about their true position. Her insight gives a revelatory explanation of how we as women can enter the true essence of leadership in balance.

Sheila White
Author, *Discovering Your Uniqueness*
Vice President, Road 2 Eternity Production Co.

In *Eve, Where Are You?* Dr. Nicole L. Davis draws upon her many years of experience as a navy veteran, a church leader, an academic scholar, and a successful entrepreneur to provide a working blueprint for other women who wish to pursue leadership opportunities in both the church and the marketplace. What makes *Eve, Where Are You?* a must-read is Dr. Davis's powerful personal journey of overcoming a dysfunctional single-parent childhood that ultimately resulted in her owning her authentic voice and embracing a higher calling. Furthermore, she masterfully weaves her stories with compelling insights from her study of prominent women in both the church and the marketplace. Dr. Davis dispels the illusion that the church and marketplace are mutually exclusive but rather can be one and the same, especially for women who are in the position to initiate positive change. Dr. Davis argues that a woman's success derives as much from those who applaud her as well as those who reject her. She also maintains that these factors are critical components to the stability of a woman's self-confidence, which can affect how she cultivates her personal identity. *Eve, Where Are You?* provides a significant contribution to the theory and practice of conflict resolution, business leadership, and the navigation of a historically patriarchal church system.

Kacey Shap, PhD
Research Consultant & Cofounder, Ology Research Group

Eve,

Where Are You?

Confronting Toxic Practices Against
the Advancement of Women

Nicole L. Davis, PhD

WESTBOW
PRESS®
A DIVISION OF THOMAS NELSON
& ZONDERVAN

WestBow Press books may be ordered through booksellers or by contacting:

WestBow Press
A Division of Thomas Nelson & Zondervan
1663 Liberty Drive
Bloomington, IN 47403
www.westbowpress.com
844-714-3454

Cover Image Credit
Sarah Grace

ISBN: 978-1-6642-0636-6 (sc)
ISBN: 978-1-6642-0638-0 (hc)
ISBN: 978-1-6642-0637-3 (e)

Library of Congress Control Number: 2020918308

Print information available on the last page.

WestBow Press rev. date: 11/18/2020

To every woman who feels deep within her soul that God requires more than she is currently giving in service to him.

To every spiritual leader who has the extraordinary responsibility of overseeing a church organization and is now sensing the need to advance the role of women.

Contents

PART 1: THE CONFLICT

PART 2: THE EXPLANATION

PART 3: THE RESOLUTION

Acknowledgments

Little did I know when I was writing my dissertation for my doctoral degree that it would result in yet another book! During that writing process, I was keenly aware there was still more that needed to be said far beyond the research I had conducted. The willingness, strength, wisdom, insight, courage, and passion to complete this project came directly from the Lord. He literally breathed this vision into me and gave me everything I needed to write and produce a quality product for women, whom he fiercely adores! I am forever grateful that God would allow me the honor of serving him in this way. I have come to learn that God absolutely *loves* his creation, woman, and everything she represents. I take great pleasure in being a spokesperson to remind women of their standing in Christ. He gave his very life so that she can walk intimately with him throughout her life and leadership. I thank God for doing *all* of this!

I want to applaud and thank my family of men. My fellas are the *bomb*! My husband and sons have challenged and encouraged me in phenomenal ways that keep me excited about life, and about my contribution to this world as a woman. They treat me like a queen and a soldier. The way they believe in me is a gift, and I'm eternally grateful for it. We are truly a unit. Thank you, Tony, Jay, and Josh—the Davis men.

Thank you to my best friend, Lenora, my ISI (iron sharpening iron) sister! We have spent many years of long hours talking, dreaming, and planning our steps to fulfill God's assignments for our lives. We never could quite figure out his ways, but the ride has been oh, so sweet. You have made this journey special and memorable with many tears and a whole bunch of laughter!

Let me also shout out Natasha, my writing coach. You helped me bring this book to life by teaching me to reach deep inside to deliver my heart. You were the right one, baby! Additionally, thank you to those who endorsed this book. You have all walked closely with me in various seasons. God used you to pull out the gems that were buried deep within. I would have never discovered the varying degrees of *me* without you.

Finally, to every man, woman, child, family member, friend, associate, and fan who has inspired me along the way, thank you for your love and your support. Let's keep doing this work together until every woman is shining in her own God-given light.

Ephesians 2:1–10 (NIV)

As for you, you were dead in your transgressions and sins, in which you used to live when you followed the ways of this world and of the ruler of the kingdom of the air, the spirit who is now at work in those who are disobedient. All of us also lived among them at one time, gratifying the cravings of our flesh and following its desires and thoughts. Like the rest, we were by nature deserving of wrath. But because of his great love for us, God, who is rich in mercy, made us alive with Christ even when we were dead in transgressions—it is by grace you have been saved. And God raised us up with Christ and seated us with him in the heavenly realms in Christ Jesus, in order that in the coming ages he might show the incomparable riches of his grace, expressed in his kindness to us in Christ Jesus. For it is by grace you have been saved, through faith—and this is not from yourselves, it is the gift of God—not by works, so that no one can boast. *For we are God's handiwork, created in Christ Jesus to do good works, which God prepared in advance for us to do.* (emphasis added)

O Man, Hear the Heart of a Woman

It's hard being a woman. We did not choose to carry your seed. God fashioned us with a womb to do so. We did not choose our gifts and callings. God assigned them to us.

We struggle with accepting who we are, and we would prefer not to fight with you about who we are. Many women try to take the path of least resistance—to be fine with working, going home, and enjoying their families—but, God said, "Not so."

Men, we need your protection, your prayers, and your pronouncement over us that we are loved and accepted. We are not your enemy. You do not have to fear our strength. The secret to our advancement, our might as the church, and as the body of Christ is our unity.

We are in the same battle as you. We are warriors too. God will not allow us to be denied the right to serve him just as you do.

Written by Dr. Nicole L. Davis

His Foreword

Eve, Where Are You? by Nicole Davis is a book that goes beyond women's liberation or feminism gone amuck. It is a doctrinal, well-researched, and practically challenging treatise for every man and woman of God who wants to see the kingdom of God working as it should on the earth. The liberating of women in church leadership is not a left-leaning, feminist idea. It is a biblical framing that God himself arranged. Because the wrecking ball of sin has damaged the union and communion between men and women, the idea of cogender leadership within the church can seem like an extreme idea or political agenda creeping into God's house.

Nicole Davis aptly puts before the reader a clear case for why women have had to fight through the quicksand of low self-identity, male-dominated culture, and church discrimination. For women who feel that the call of God on their lives is to fully express their God-given gifts in the church, many have had to fight and claw their way into service, not only against men but against the resistance of women too. For called and qualified women of God, many have had to wait, pray, and hope that one day those in authority, such as myself, would see the light of God's design and plan for their deployment.

As the senior pastor and founder of Bridgeway Community Church in Columbia, Maryland, and in Owings Mills - Reisterstown, Maryland, I have always believed that women could serve in leadership under my covering. In fact, I still do. But to my chagrin, I slow walked the process of women being ordained. I am sorry it took me so long.

While we established the Women's Development Leadership

Institute (WLDI) a dozen years ago, licensed women to preach more than fifteen years ago, and had women leading some of our largest ministries, ordaining women as pastors was not a reality. Having women on our management team over the last decade and having established an Elders Council of Women (ECW) to walk with the male elders of the church to give spiritual oversight to the church, we still had no ordination of women pastors. Over the last two years, it was clear that the time was coming. My heart and spirit were growing more courageous. My tolerance for all male pastors and the shutting out of female pastors was just not acceptable to me any longer. Concern that I might lose pastors, church members, or other staff was no longer a sufficient excuse for me to not pursue breaking this glass ceiling at Bridgeway.

Having approached all three of our female ministers about becoming pastors, one felt the call to begin the quiet process of preparing for this inevitable calling on her life in earnest. I had also been preparing the elders behind the scenes. In addition, I had been preparing the church without them even realizing it. Having women preachers as a regular part of our preaching rotation for a decade and teaching character studies on women like Sheerah, Esther, Ruth, and others, it was time to make the big move and prepare myself for the consequences of ordaining this amazingly qualified woman to be our first female pastor. Talking our male clergy through the process and teaching our elders the word of God on the matter took a while, but the time was now.

On January 26, 2020, our church celebrated the ordaining of a lovely, Spirit-filled, gifted, and called woman who had striven with our ministry for years. This woman reached out to Nicole Davis so she could watch the service online since Nicole and her husband had moved their membership elsewhere and hadn't been a part of our church for a few years. Nicole's heart was personally moved. And why wouldn't she be? Her journey of trying to lead well in churches throughout her adult life was an evolving battle, as you will read in this book. I am sure she was wondering if her gifts would ever be fully realized.

You will see in *Eve, Where Are You?* how God is fulfilling

her every dream and utilizing Nicole Davis's gifts to advance the kingdom of God. I pray that your eye-opening and heart-affirming journey of seeing women for all God has created them to be increases as you turn the page and read every word of *Eve, Where Are You?*

Dr. David A. Anderson
Senior pastor and Founder, Bridgeway Community Church

Her Foreword

This book is riveting. I began reading it at two o'clock in the morning and couldn't put it down. I was exhausted, yet I was determined to allow the Holy Spirit to do a deep work in me as I was reading it. Dr. Nicole Davis has selflessly and for no self-aggrandizement written this book for the purpose of liberating the thinking of many people—men and women. I read voraciously to get every morsel of this gut-level truth being presented here by Dr. Nicole. This book is transformative because it very simply reveals the stinkin' thinkin' that has shackled women's minds since birth and is insidiously squeezing out (like a python) our desire for leadership. As a matter of fact, this demonic process started with Eve not accepting God's purpose for her life relative to Adam and God himself.

Only a woman such as Dr. Nicole qualifies to write this very weighty truth because her integrity matches her deep desire for God's truth. Very few Christians are willing to enter into the fellowship of Jesus's suffering as Nicole has done to know him in this revelatory fashion. Though her journey has been hard, and I know because I had the privilege to watch and be a colaborer with her during a very spiritually challenging time of her journey, it is evident that she persevered for a time such as this. Most Christians want the power of Jesus's resurrection but want to take shortcuts, which is why their anointing is weak, and in some cases, it appears nonexistent. I've had the honor to know Nicole for almost two decades when her daily quest was to understand her purpose because she instinctively knew that God had much more for her. Her famous question at that time was *why*. However, she was in the process of being broken (crushed) and getting prepared for this amazing conflict resolution ministry that is so needed for her to compassionately serve many people that she will walk with through their hurts, pain, and rejections. This is how servants are made.

I highly recommend this book to men, women, and teenagers so they can learn how to press into the grace of God to endure the pain, suffering, and shame of the cross to find joy in this life. There is joy in knowing that our lives are not our own and that we can be trusted by God to bring souls out of darkness into his marvelous light as Nicole does daily. God trusts his servant Nicole to do this very special job because he knows that Nicole will give him the glory, honor, and praise for the great things he is doing and shall do in her life.

Apostle Gail A. Addison
President/CEO, End Time Harvest Ministries

A Letter of Admiration from My Husband

Dear Nicole,

When we met in the navy, you were a young, exciting breath of fresh air who was seeking to extract all of the benefits of life. Your captivating personality, coupled with your attention to detail and excellence, has catapulted you to leadership positions despite your preferred desire to stay off the radar. You've helped many people behind the scenes. The interactions were private, and that was exactly the way you liked it. Fanfare was unnecessary. Agreement from others was certainly unnecessary. And a platform where you would champion a cause as a trailblazer was unnecessary and just a downright pointless proposition. You were (and still are) the ultimate paradox. You are a passionate person who would prefer to stay low key. I want to commend you for having the intestinal fortitude to address this critical and polarizing topic. When it was placed on your heart to "care" about this topic, you chose to take action.

Regardless of how it's expressed, everyone wants to feel valued. We need to feel like our lives have some meaning. We often ask ourselves in some sort of way, "Who am I, why was I born, and what am I going to do now that I am here?" Consequently, many people often explore the teachings of religion to search for these answers. This search has led many to transform their lives. Unfortunately, at the same time, many religious teachings have yielded answers that leave women unfulfilled. They embrace their liberating discoveries, only to live in cultures that tell them that such liberties are not designed for them. As a result, women try to convince themselves to conform to teachings and practices that oppose the truth that resides inside them. To make matters worse, these women are often left to fight alone because they are not able to obtain an adequate support system from the men who love them and the religious systems that supposedly want them to be all that God has created them to be.

With this book, you have provided the answer to questions asked and unasked. You have done it even with the title of this book. While it appears to be another question, *Eve, Where Are You?* is actually a rallying cry to help women stand up. It's also a challenge to them to recognize obstacles and either rise above them or simply destroy them—just choose to no longer accept them. Ultimately, it's an encouraging reminder that "all things are possible" is more than just a nice religious cliché.

Thank you for liberating the minds of everyone who reads this book. The words and stories contained herein challenge everyone to explore and revisit traditional cultural teachings. For women who have abdicated their significance, they will find the courage to take it back and become the best versions of themselves. At the same time, men who read this book will look at their wives and daughters with increased value and a heightened sense of purpose. If they allow themselves to do so, they will want to make sure that the *real* her has an opportunity to be manifested to the world.

It's not uncommon for us to call our wives queens and our daughters our little princesses. Now, through your book, we'll have some understanding to support her in her royalty. As we do that at home, those traits will extend to the other women in our lives and in our circles of influence as well.

I love you for being unapologetically you. Stay faithful to your call because the world needs what's in you.

Many hugs and kisses and hugs and kisses.
Tony

Introduction

"So how was the partnership class?" I asked my son.

"It was okay," he answered.

He then gave me the rundown on the meeting's highlights. Little did I know that as he continued to talk, the trajectory of my life would be changed forever. Let me explain a little about my background before I continue this story.

My two younger sisters and I grew up in a single-parent home. Even though my mom and dad were in an on-again-off-again relationship for over thirty years, they were never married. In watching the dysfunctional dynamics of my parents' relationship, I vowed to never get married. My dad was a thief, a drug dealer, and a drug user. He was in and out of jail. I disdained everything he represented, and I resented my mother for allowing him to continually come in and out of our lives. I grew up angry, bitter, and reckless in my decision-making. I had no respect for my parents, and I had no respect for myself. I made careless decisions that were priming me to follow in my mother's footsteps without even realizing it. I was the textbook example of what it meant to be the product of a broken home. As a result, I had broken thoughts, and I lived a broken life, emotionally, relationally, mentally, and spiritually.

I know what it's like to visit a parent in prison; I know what it's like to live on public assistance; I know what it's like to live in poor conditions; and I know what it's like to feel like life is unfair and cruel. Even though these dark things were my reality growing up, something inside of me wouldn't allow me to stop hoping for better. I knew as soon as I turned eighteen, to give myself a fighting chance, I had to leave my hometown and everything that was familiar to me, so I did. As I type these words to share about a situation that occurred with one of my sons, it's sometimes hard to believe I have been blessed with such an amazing life and family of my own. My husband of almost thirty years and I have two adult sons, and my relationships with them are in stark contrast with how I was raised. I never envisioned any of this for myself. It's a constant reminder that God has more for us than what we can ever conceive for ourselves. Now, back to the story.

Our elder son had just completed his undergraduate degree at a prestigious Ivy League school before moving back home. A yearlong background check had to be completed before he was to move to another city and start his new job. While in college, our son had been away from our home church. Upon his return, he registered to attend the new partnership class to decide for himself if he wanted to continue attending the same church. Although our family held memberships at the church for four years, our son wanted to determine if this ministry was still right for him now that he was an adult. By this time, we were very active members there. My husband was a leader with the men's care ministry. Our younger son was heavily involved with the youth ministry and the technology department. I was the director of the women's ministry, responsible for developing programming for thousands of women. Our family finally felt comfortable and settled. Getting to this point in our church life had been a miraculous move of God.

It began when our younger son, who was attending Christian school, reached eighth grade. He shared with us that he wanted to start going to church because his friends from school all attended churches. Upon his request, we reluctantly decided to start visiting churches. Our past experiences with churches and church leadership had left a bad taste in our mouths. Both my husband and I had become quite content with sending our children to Christian school, while we watched Christian television to get our dose of sermons. With us both being military veterans, we were accustomed to being in regions around the world where church services were unavailable or where we had to create small gatherings with fellow Christians as a way to support one another with prayer and Bible studies. From our various experiences, we believed staying away from church involvement was the best way to stay out of trouble with church folks.

The particular church that we eventually ended up joining had been recommended to us years prior, but at that time, we had no desire to visit. Once we decided to give it a try, to our surprise, the church was big and lively, and the boys loved the ministries offered for middle schoolers and high schoolers. Initially, my husband and I decided since the boys enjoyed it, we would attend, but we had no plans of becoming members or getting actively involved. We wanted to stay under the radar, and we didn't want anyone to know that we were ordained ministers from a previous church. We figured we would continue attending services at this church until our younger son graduated high school. Once he went off to college, our plan was to go back to the solace of our home ministry and resume watching TV church.

Because of my past painful church experiences, I made a deal with God: if he wanted me to be involved with church ministry in any way, he would have to bring the opportunities to me. I had decided I was not going to put myself out there anymore by speaking out, for fear of mistreatment, and I was not going to volunteer to be a part of anything. I was too afraid of what the outcome would be if I got involved again. Also, I didn't want to deal with people's misinterpretations of my motives because in the past I'd been accused of trying to change things, and of trying to "be seen." This had been a regular occurrence whenever I questioned how something was done or offered suggestions for improvements.

Once we decided to attend this new church, I knew I didn't want to deal with being accused of being *rebellious* or a *Jezebel*, which are terms commonly reserved for assertive women. These are criticisms I had heard before. By this point in my life, I was clear: I only wanted what God wanted for me, or so I thought. What I really wanted was self-preservation. I intentionally ignored and dismissed all spiritual gifts, skills, and instinctive and perceptive abilities I possessed. I had come to learn that these attributes had gotten me in trouble with insecure male church leaders and competitive women church leaders. I just didn't want any more trouble. Although I had been told many times over the years by church members and leaders that I was a leader and that God had a call on my life, I wasn't willing to share any of that information with anyone at this new church. As a result of past hurts, I told God that if he wanted me in a leadership role, he'd have to drop it into my lap, and I meant it.

It wasn't long before my curiosity caused me to attend a couple of women's events. I was interested to know if these women really trusted in God's word and were serious about their faith. Learning and talking about the power of God and his word has always been my favorite way to fellowship with other Christians, and I longed to have those kinds of in-depth conversations with my new Christian sisters. I was pleasantly surprised once I allowed myself to get involved. Not only did I enjoy the women, but I also found many of them to be spiritually powerful, knowledgeable, wise, loving, giving, and fun! Still, I remained cautious and somewhat guarded. I never revealed that I was an ordained minister or any of my other credentials. Though at times, my compassion for people couldn't be abated, and I would find myself speaking encouraging words to hurting and emotionally broken women or fervently praying for someone when I sensed a need. Naturally, this attracted unwanted attention. But staying under the radar was still my goal, so I shied away from probing questions about myself as best I could.

My husband and I eventually had to join the church so that the boys could have full access to all the activities and opportunities offered by their youth ministries. Part of the requirement for partnership was volunteering with a church ministry of our choice. To fulfill this requirement, I decided to join the women's care group. I liked it because I could help other women. To my surprise, while still in the early phase of taking the required classes to become a qualified volunteer with this ministry team, out of the blue, I was contacted by one of the senior group leaders and told that God led her to ask me to be one of the incoming leaders! I was shocked yet amused at how quickly God dropped a leadership role right "into my lap!" I had only been around these women on a couple of occasions, so it seemed unimaginable that they would've asked me to lead so quickly. Not to mention, there were dozens of other women who were already serving with this ministry, so I was baffled how I would have been able to be considered before them.

But because of my deal with God, I accepted the offer to lead. I loved the fact that God honored the requirements that I asked of him regarding my willingness to get involved. He met me where I was, and I was thankful for his patience with me in this area. \

Shortly thereafter, within a year's time, and during our third year attending this church, greater responsibility beckoned. I was recruited to be the director of the women's ministry! I was asked to lead the largest ministry the church offered. I was completely blown away. I was told that, up to that point of them asking *me* with less than four years at the church, the position had been held by the pastor's wife and other long-standing senior women in the church. I didn't even know the church's senior leadership knew who I was! When I was contacted by one of the male church leaders, he told me that my name kept coming up as they were seeking God and talking to other church leaders about the next person to appoint to lead the women. I mention this not to brag or crown myself with a diadem of specialty, no. I mention this because it drives home the reality that God uses whom he chooses, but he also expects our obedience. When God calls you into leadership, you can run away from it, but you can't hide.

God was demonstrating right before my eyes that even though I thought I was hidden, I was not. And even though I thought people did not see me, I was seen. I marveled at the doors that God was opening so quickly for me. It was scary! I had worked so hard over the years, telling myself that it didn't matter what I did, whether I showed up, or if I said anything. While I thought I was controlling what was happening to me, God was in control all along. I remember God impressing upon my heart that up to that point, he had accommodated my desire to raise our children and live under the radar, but now he was showing me that he needed me to come out from the back—no more hiding in the dark. Astonished and humbled, I accepted the position. Now back to the story about my son.

As I listened to my son's reaction to certain information he received in the new partnership class he'd attended, I tried to gauge his acceptance or rejection of what he had heard. "Mom," he said, "they don't believe women can lead without being under the authority of a man. Plus, they don't have any women pastors."

My head nod gave him the permission to continue talking. I had no clue where the conversation was going, but I sensed that things would soon begin to unravel. "I didn't know this church doesn't believe in ordaining women pastors," he said. "As I was listening to them speak, I was thinking, *Mom and Dad are okay with this*?" I felt sick. My neck and head were getting warmer as I rummaged through my mind as to how best to answer him.

"Yes, I know about the church's stance on women." I shrugged my shoulders. "It never mattered to me though," I continued. "I didn't care because ... it wasn't like I was looking to get ordained."

My son looked intently at me, searching for a reason to accept what I was saying. I felt gut-punched. He basically was calling me out for accepting something that I didn't believe in, and I'd disappointed him because I was willing to give in to a doctrine that didn't align with our family values or with the Bible. We taught our children that it's important to treat *everyone* with respect; that we must *all* work hard to get what we want; that God has a calling on *all* our lives. We *all* have a part to play in accomplishing the assignment God has for us, and that there are never any distinctions made between the level, importance, or complexity of assignments given to men over women. It was my own selfishness that caused me to tell my son that it was okay to look past our church's stance on women in the pulpit. Simply put, that was the wrong response.

"Well *now*, I need you to *care*." I heard *his* voice boom inside my head. Instinctively, I knew it was God. The statement paralyzed me. In that instance I knew God was requiring more of me. He wanted me to care at a deeper level about the plight of women in his church: their growth, their identity, their emotional stability, and their understanding of their unique purpose and destiny.

My son continued to share his displeasure. His lips were moving, but I could not, however, hear his words because for a brief moment, my mind transcended to an internal conversation with God. My son did not know what was happening. God had set me up! He took this opportunity to use my son to get my undivided attention. God was letting me know he needed me to work for *him*—not just to think of myself as a volunteer at a church building. Working for him meant a life dedicated to his service, whether I attended a church or not. He wanted my focus to be the advancement of his kingdom, not only the advancement of a pastor's mission and vision.

During our internal conversation, God reminded me of the time he told me to surrender to his plan, and to accept that my life was marked for leadership. His role for me was to be in front, not in the back, not only as a passive member but as an active pioneer of something better. It was *his* plan that I be willing to take more responsibility as his representative in the earth; otherwise, if I chose not to accept his plan for me, I would continue to live a frustrated life.

God already knows I possess a burning desire to see him represented with excellence and integrity since he formed me with it; and, that it is important to me that *everyone* feel valued, no matter who they are. I desire to see things done with class, civility, respect, and timeliness. I am a huge proponent of delivering services to others with special attention to detail and order. God had told me and demonstrated so many times that I was not "regular," and I would not be fulfilled trying to live a regular life.

For years I had tried to ignore that inner pull I periodically felt. I hoped to attain contentment at various stages in my life as a stay-at-home mother, as a good friend, as a loving wife, and as a faithful church volunteer, and these are all admirable positions in life. But God kept reminding me, "I have need of you. There is more that I want to do through your life." Over and over I wouldn't accept that. I just didn't believe it. Why me? After all, who was I? What did I really matter? And I often questioned his selection of me. I hadn't been raised in church, and I didn't act churchy, so why leadership? I never wanted the extra responsibilities. Still I couldn't seem to avoid them. I'd say to God, "You have others who are certainly more qualified who are willing to lead and speak for you." I tried many times to reason with him. But on this day, while talking to my son, it became agonizingly obvious to me that God was no longer entertaining my pleas. This was finally my day of reckoning.

In the deep recesses of my heart, I finally relented, realizing I was really clueless about who he had fashioned me to be—which had been determined long before I was born. Consequently, in that moment and on *that* day, while talking to my son it was clear that I was to step fully into God's calling for me—come out of the shadows and stop doing just enough to feel good about serving him. God wanted to know where I stood regarding my commitment to him. He wanted me to give him a deep and eternal yes. He wanted my trust, along with a loyal and unconditional yes—a yes that didn't require him to reveal his full plan for me up front. A faith-filled yes. "It's time," God said to me. And I knew he was no longer accepting any of my excuses. It was a profound moment because I discerned that it wasn't just time for me alone anymore. He was saying, "It's time for *women*."

The topic of female leadership in the church has been a source of great debate for centuries. I for one was not interested in the debate. I accepted the status quo that men were the leader and women the follower, yet I never internalized the limitations directed toward women embedded in that ideology. When I was a new Christian, I was under the impression that pastors were supposed to be men. I thought this way because all I had ever been exposed to were male senior pastors. I saw women taking on leadership positions in other capacities within the church, but I never seriously considered them as occupying the role as a senior pastor. I accepted the idea of copastors with a husband and wife pastoring together, yet I still saw the husband as the primary leader. What I was exposed to definitely skewed my thinking about women as church leaders. I remember having conversations about whether I would be willing to sit under a female pastor, and the answer was a swift no. There were a couple of churches in our geographical region with women senior pastors, and it just seemed to be a rare exception to the rule. I wasn't against it. Women could pastor if they wanted to; I just didn't want to attend a church led by one.

The issues regarding the devaluation and rejection of female church leaders became more real the moment my son challenged me that fateful Sunday afternoon. My life has not been the same. From my son's single question, I have made some significant moves in my life. I pursued a doctorate in conflict analysis and resolution and studied the impact of the patriarchal system on gender imbalance and how various female pastors overcame the stigma that I came to accept as facts of life. I changed churches and was soon thereafter ordained to function as an associate pastor. I cofounded Empower to Engage with my husband where we provide leadership and personal development resources, training, coaching, and consulting in the areas of marriage, parenting, and organizational leadership; and, we've coauthored several books.

As a woman, a pastor, and a marketplace leader, I can now fully recognize my value and ministry opportunities in all of these areas. Godly ministry operates in many forms and in many spheres of influence, whether sanctioned within a church or private institution. Knowing this, I cannot allow myself to get lost in the opinions of others. It is God whom I desire to please, and I've learned that he needs the women he calls to show up and step into the light. He needs women to accept a seat at the table. He needs women to take their position in the battle for our families, our communities, our churches, and society at large. It is time for the woman's role to equal a man's role in relevance and acceptance at the highest levels. And God needs women to represent him well no matter where we are or what we are doing anywhere we are in the world. What does this mean regarding how we as women live and move about the earth? Only you can answer these questions as they pertain to your own life.

Since I understand that God has given me skills, abilities, and talents for his use, it has changed the way I conduct myself. I fully understand that he expects much from me because I'm made in his image and his likeness. I no longer accept boundaries or man-sanctioned limitations on what I can be or accomplish because I know who God is in me. Can you say the same? If you're not sure, I ask the question, Eve, where are *you*?

Eve is every woman who has lived, loved, and dreamed. Eve represents every nationality, creed, and color. Eve is succeeding and failing, yet she still needs to discover her full identity. Eve is bold sometimes and fearful at others. Eve is the woman who needs to experience her next level of greatness. Eve is me. Eve is you. The question is a real one that deserves a solid answer. This is not just *my* story; this is our collective story.

Women have to find their voices and make choices that matter primarily to the one looking back at them in the mirror. It is not my desire to present the information in this book as a womanist or feminist. I simply believe in the equality of women and the right for women to be able to fully accomplish any goal or career aspiration they desire. I have no plan to create a she-woman man haters club. Although there are women who would like to believe we rule the world, men are just as powerful as we are. No one can convince me otherwise. I love, respect, and need men. Let me state that again. I *love, respect,* and *need* men. I have been blessed to have a husband and two sons who have been the biggest supporters of my work. It is a testament that God's desire is that men and women care deeply for one another and value one another's place in this world.

This labor of love is based on my doctoral dissertation entitled *Women in Ministry: How Conflicts Between God's Purpose and Church Doctrine Impact the Efficacy of Female Church Leaders.* I will be sharing the lives, stories, and beliefs of both male and female church leaders who participated in my study. From their perspectives, you will learn more deeply what the challenges are that the Christian church has ahead. More importantly, you will better understand how significant you are in repairing the breaches between man and woman, woman and herself, and woman and the Christian church. The research participants consisted of twelve church leaders made up of six women and six men. Two women and two men leaders were selected from three different Christian church denominations: a nondenominational church, a Baptist church that recently converted to being a nondenominational church, and an African Methodist Episcopal (AME) Zion Church.

Let me forewarn you: this book is not for everyone. This is a revolutionary, challenging call to action for women who want more, men who want more for women, and church organizations that want to embrace the need for transformation within their ranks.

In this book you will hear the hearts and the struggles of men and women grappling with the topic of women in leadership. These are the people I met as I studied the conflict between God's purpose and church doctrine regarding women in leadership. This topic is a hard one, no doubt. But we must have the conversation. We must address the reality that there are those, both men and women, who insist on creating barriers of entry for women in leadership. It's still occurring in great numbers within our churches. The questions we must ask beyond denominational, cultural, and independent scriptural interpretations are: (1) Why are we holding on to a belief that is so divisive and oppressive to one gender?, (2) What needs to be done to make sure everyone feels valued and fulfilled in the body of Christ? and, (3) How can women get their spiritual, personal, and professional needs met by attending Christian church? Collectively, we have the answers, but these solutions are dormant, awaiting to be discovered and activated. If we don't unify, what will be the ultimate cost to the effectiveness and relevance of the church? Let's begin the journey of unleashing brilliance, talent, wisdom, and individual self-efficacy. The woman is the focus of this endeavor.

This book is divided into three parts. Part 1, "The Conflict," I examine facets of the gender conflict and why it is necessary to address them for the advancement of women, the church, and ultimately the kingdom of God. You will meet the participants from my research who give voice to the varying opinions regarding whether women should hold positions of authority. You will learn where their thoughts about women originated and how those thoughts have been lived out in both the church and the marketplace.

Part 2, "The Explanation," I discuss the various causes that keep our churches entrenched in this battle of the sexes. I analyze the role of *identity* and how the marginalization of women has caused widespread apathy among women. The *power* struggle and how this is impacting the resistance of men including women as viable church leadership. Finally, I look at the influence of our mental mapping and our willingness and unwillingness to *change* based on perceived ideologies and learned behavior.

In part 3, "The Resolution," I outline the R.E.F.R.E.S.H.® model as a nontraditional approach to developing women and restructuring churches to admirably address gendered transgression. This model has been designed to help women find ways to utilize their gifts in both the church and the marketplace. I also discuss ways for churches to support women which can enhance the vitality of the church, as men and women *colabor* for the upbuilding of God's kingdom at every level. The R.E.F.R.E.S.H.® model supports church organizations that are ready to take the plunge to totally and completely re-present how church will operate in decades to come, to include both men and women at the highest levels of function and authority.

So much effort and energy has been utilized against women for far too long. Critical action is required right now. It's time to redirect our focus and begin concentrating on strengthening, encouraging, and equipping women to take their rightful place in both the church and the marketplace as joint heirs and *corulers* here on earth—all to the glory of God. This journey is not for the faint of heart. It requires us to open our minds and be willing to relinquish our biases so we can relearn. It requires a soul and a spirit that seeks to unite instead of divide. It requires an inclusive worldview that seeks for the righteous response to the needs of humanity. No one person can do it all, nor can one gender. The time is now for leaders to arise from the four corners of the earth. Men have taken their position and served heroically. When God spoke in the garden of Eden that male and female were to rule and reign over the earth *together*, we've predominantly seen only the man in position. So I ask again … Eve, where are *you*?

PART 1

The Conflict

*Sometimes God doesn't send you into a
battle to win it; He sends you to end it.*
—Shannon L. Alder

Chapter 1

Marketplace Opportunities vs. Church Opportunities

The World Applauds Me, but I'm Rejected by My Own

*B*efore I begin this chapter, let me present you with three loaded questions.

As a woman, what do *you* do when you, (1) have a passion or a sense of duty to *be* something or to *do* something that may be contrary to what others think is right for you (those others could be a boss, a coworker, a business partner, a family member, a professor, a pastor, a friend, or even your spouse); (2) have a burden to go after a skill, a vocation, a career, a business, or anything else that you have been taught is flat out wrong for you to have—so it causes you to doubt yourself; or (3) believe in your heart that you have been born to pursue a cause beyond your capacity or current abilities?

Of course, there are no easy answers to these questions, and the path to discovering how you should respond may be riddled with pain, frustration, and uncertainty. I can attest that these are emotions I've felt on my journey. It's exactly what I went through to successfully find myself where I am today: feeling free, fulfilled, excited about my life, and excited about the assignment God has given me. To be able to finally stand in this place, knowing who I am, with the confidence and courage to face the unknown, I say, without hesitation, that I would go through it all again.

As a woman pursues leadership opportunities—whether it's within religious organizations as a deacon, elder, pastor, or higher, or in the marketplace as a supervisor, director, chief executive officer, or owner of her own enterprise—who applauds her and who rejects her can become critical components to the stability of her self-confidence, and ultimately to the clarity she possesses (or not), which affects how she cultivates her personal identity.

Your Worldview Matters

The conflict we wrestle with regarding who and what we are as women is multidimensional. Its origin, with debatable nuances and interpretations, began in the garden of Eden, where we are shown the following: God's creation of humankind, God's guidance and instructions given to man and woman for living, and the subsequent fall when man and woman disobeyed God. I am a firm believer in the Bible, and I believe in creationism, so the reality that humankind began with Adam and Eve influences my worldview. It is also important for you to know what *you* believe about how humankind showed up on this planet and God's original plan for us because it's the foundation for how you resolve who you are, where you come from (besides your mommy's tummy), why you're here, and what you are capable of accomplishing and possessing. Genesis 1:26–28 (NIV) states:

> Then God said, "Let us make mankind in our image, in our likeness, so that they may rule over the fish in the sea and the birds in the sky, over the livestock and all the wild animals, and over all the creatures that move along the ground." So God created mankind in his own image, in the image of God he created them; male and female he created them. God blessed them and said to them,

"Be fruitful and increase in number; fill the earth and subdue it. Rule over the fish in the sea and the birds in the sky and over every living creature that moves on the ground."

From the beginning woman was given the same authority as man. God established a model where man and woman would have dominion over the earth together, not dominion over one another (which is one dimension of the conflict). In Genesis 2, the Bible describes God creating "a helper comparable to him," referring to Eve being taken from Adam's side, thus being fashioned as a suitable mate. The interpretation of the word *helper* is another dimension of the conflict. The Hebrew meaning of this word, *ezer*, means protector or rescuer. The same word is used in describing God and the Holy Spirit. It's not meant to be interpreted or enforced as one who is subordinate or inferior. The Bible continuously corroborates God's stern instruction concerning respecting the powerbase of the woman in both the Old and New Testament. In Proverbs 18:22, God's word admonishes, "He that finds a wife finds a good thing and obtains favor from the Lord" (NKJV). In 1 Peter 3:7 (NKJV), it says, "Husbands, likewise, dwell with them with understanding, giving honor to the wife as to the weaker vessel, and as being heirs together of the grace of life; that your prayers may not be hindered." Both scriptures stress that women are so powerful that they automatically bring favor from God into your life, and the mistreatment of them can cause significant hindrance to your prayers. But when these scriptures are preached from male-dominated pulpits, the emphasis is put on women needing to wait until they are *found* by a man and that they are (physically) weaker than men and subordinate. Though these scriptures pertain to marriage, their importance in establishing the godly authority of women in God's kingdom on the earth is immense.

The Bible also explains the fall of humankind, where the conflict began between man and woman. This ongoing discussion about Adam and Eve serves as yet another dimension of the conflict because Eve, who now represents all women, is continually penalized for the ultimate sin that both Adam and Eve succumbed to together. Genesis 3:8–13 (NIV) states:

Then the man and his wife heard the sound of the Lord God as he was walking in the garden in the cool of the day, and they hid from the Lord God among the trees of the garden. But the Lord God called to the man, "Where are you?" He answered, "I heard you in the garden, and I was afraid because I was naked; so I hid." And he said, "Who told you that you were naked? Have you eaten from the tree that I commanded you not to eat from?" The man said, "The woman you put here with me—she gave me some fruit from the tree, and I ate it." Then the Lord God said to the woman, "What is this you have done?" The woman said, "The serpent deceived me, and I ate."

The resulting consequences are outlined in Genesis 3:14–21(NIV), which reads,

So the Lord God said to the serpent, "Because you have done this, "Cursed are you above all livestock and all wild animals! You will crawl on your belly and you will eat dust all the days of your life. And I will put enmity between you and the woman, and between your offspring and hers; he will crush your head, and you will strike his heel." To the woman he said, "I will make your pains in childbearing very severe; with painful labor you will give birth to children. Your desire will be for your husband, and he will rule over you." To Adam he said, "Because you listened to your wife and ate fruit from the tree about which I commanded you, 'You must not eat from it,' Cursed is the ground because of you; through painful toil you will eat food from it all the days of your life. It will produce thorns and thistles for you, and you will eat the plants of the field. By the sweat of your brow you will eat your food until you return to the ground, since from it you were taken; for dust you are and to dust you

will return." Adam named his wife Eve, because
she would become the mother of all the living. The
Lord God made garments of skin for Adam and his
wife and clothed them.

The edict from God that followed Adam and Eve's decision
to eat of the forbidden fruit is the premise of the conflict that
permeates church doctrine, along with the false beliefs about
women and their right to assume or not to assume leadership
in the church today. We have subsequently maligned various
scriptures against women to perpetually justify subjugating and
marginalizing them with erroneous depictions of her role both at
home and in the church. However, this bias against women is not
as easily permissible in the marketplace as in times past. In fact,
it's now illegal to limit women based on gender in many areas of
society in the United States, because of Title VII.[1]

Gifts and Talents are Transferrable

Although the Bible tells us how we began in the garden of Eden,
our present situation of combating the glass (and sometimes steel)
ceiling in our churches pales when reflecting the power found in
the ultimate sacrifice that Jesus made for all of us on the cross
of Calvary. He redeemed and restored humankind, both men and
women, back to a right relationship with him, and once again gave
us total access to every promise, as well as all authority originally
assigned to the man and the woman. We are both made in the
image and likeness of God.

The conflict, as we will engage it further, starts with a look
at the strides we've made as women in the twenty-first century.
Over the past two decades, we have witnessed the increase of
women's leadership in the secular arena. Whether it be sports,
business, education, media, or politics, we have seen a considerable
upswing in women taking top positions. Women are leveraging
their professional opportunities and realizing that they can attain
and excel at the highest levels.

What puts a damper on this phenomenal reality of women's

empowerment is that there is an internal battle that causes her to question whether she can offer the same talents that are being applauded in her career, to her local church, where she also wants to be an asset, bettering her fellow churchgoers. In fact, it is common to hear women refer to their jobs or businesses in separate terms from any ministry assignment that they may have at church. The revelation here is that the two are not necessarily mutually exclusive; they can be one in the same.

As a Christian, the kingdom and the church are in you, and they *are* you. *Kingdom of God* is defined as a way of living that represents heavenly principles and standards of God here on earth.[2] Jesus's work was to establish a kingdom way of thinking on earth, as it is in heaven. He wanted religious leaders and his followers to think with their hearts by offering mercy, compassion, and consideration of others above themselves, because the law was damaging, hurtful, and restrictive. He desired to establish a new way of coexisting that embodied servanthood and love. Our mindset about who we are, what we are doing, and what we can accomplish through God will determine whether we can also see ministry opportunities in our day-to-day line of work, no matter what it is. We can only do this successfully if we see ourselves as kingdom representatives and not only as Christians.

Gifts and callings come from God. No matter where they are utilized, whether knowingly or ignorantly, you are operating in your divine abilities when you perform. The glory and the gratitude for those gifts belong to God. It doesn't matter if you have perfected those skills in college or operate purely out of your instinctive knowhow. Why is this important? It's important because wherever you render your services, when they are properly understood and used as such, it can be ministry to the One who gave you your abilities. While we can debate how those abilities have been acquired, I believe there are no accidents in God, so he was able to get you to an expected place, occupation, skillset, and belief, by various means, both by fun or by force. He's God, he's sovereign, and it would be futile to attempt to understand his ways and his thoughts (Isaiah 55:8–9).

So that means, your writing, coaching, analytical, negotiation, administration, marketing, designing, teaching, medical, finance, legal, speaking, singing, dancing, acrobatics, athletics, problem solving, program development, information technology, joke-telling, cyber security, you name it—those gifts, talents, and abilities were divinely assigned to you as possible ministry offerings to the world. The key to allowing God to use you in this manner comes from knowing who he is and who you are in him. Gifts and abilities are not necessarily gender specific. Is that hard to believe? I'm not referring to our physical makeup where a woman may be weaker than a man of her same build, height, and weight. However, we do know there are instances where a woman can be much bigger and stronger than a man with the ability to outrun him and outlift him. Notwithstanding that fact, physiologically and reproductively speaking, there are things that only women can do, and there are things that only men can do. Neither size, age, weight, race, religion, nor socioeconomic status will change that. When you look at this list of skills and abilities, I purposefully did not put being a wife or mothering because if you are a mother or wife, those positions have been added to the gifts you were created with. Your gifts were inside of you *before* you became a mother or a wife, and they are there while you are doing those things. Thank God, those gifts are still there and can still be of use once your children become adults or should your marriage end.

Woman, there is so much to who you are. And yet, there is still so much more for you to learn about what you can do. There is no time like the present to discover, develop, and deploy your best self. It is your ministry gift to the world! If the church can grasp this reality about the woman that God fashioned in the garden of Eden, we can revolutionize how we educate, train, and utilize men and women in our churches.

Research Participants

This topic of women and specifically women in leadership is the very topic I broached with the six men and six women who participated in my research study. For the purposes of the study, their names were changed to provide confidentiality. However, their stories and their ideologies are consistent with what they shared during our interviews. Let me introduce each one of them to you.

James, Executive Pastor (Married), Caucasian, Male: James didn't grow up in the church. He came to establish his beliefs about women from reading the Bible and attending seminary. He has worked with women pastors over the years who have been strong examples and mentors to him in his leadership, and he welcomes and respects the leadership of women.

Suzanne, Elder (Married to the Church Pastor), African American, Female: Suzanne grew up in church and has attended services of various denominations. She is an advocate for capable and assertive women and believes the greatest difference between male and female leaders is their degree of competency or lack thereof. She has a background in finance and has served in leadership in church and in the marketplace.

Yvette, Elder (Married), African American, Female: Yvette grew up attending a Baptist church, but now she and her husband attend a nondenominational Caucasian church. She was a stay-at-home mom and was content being a Bible study teacher. She is the first African American woman at her church to serve in a leadership position. Her acceptance of the position brought ridicule and rejection from both her church and her family. Her husband supported her acceptance of leadership even though people criticized him for doing so.

Anna, Reverend (Married), African American, Female: Anna grew up in the Church of God in Christ denomination, where women were not allowed to be in senior pastoral roles. Many of the men she encounters still do not believe in women preachers. She worked for the federal government and held a leadership position where she competed effectively and successfully against her male counterparts.

Bill, Bishop (Married), African American, Male: Bill grew up attending a Baptist church and was taught women should not preach. He's been pastoring most of his adult life. He is transitioning his Baptist church into a nondenominational church. He says he would not debate a woman who says she's called to pastor a church; however, he would not want to sit under a female pastor even though he knows many effective female pastors. He feels some women become hardened and lose their femininity as pastors.

Cornelius, Associate Pastor (Married), African American, Male: Cornelius grew up attending a Baptist church. Women were not allowed behind the pulpit and were not allowed to teach men. Although he believes women can be strong leaders in the marketplace, he also feels that those talents do not translate to leadership qualities adequate for the church. He does not question a woman who believes she is called to pastor, but he would not want to serve under a woman. He admitted to currently serving under a woman in the marketplace for his job.

Kevin, Former Pastor (Married), Caucasian, Male: Kevin grew up as a Catholic. He had never thought about the role of women in the church. It only became a sticking point when he later served as senior pastor in a nondenominational church and wanted to have a woman teach the congregation. He was met with some resistance and confusion from the all-male elder board about the church's stance when he introduced the subject of women preachers. The debate grew into a full-blown church divide. The ultimate decision that he and the elder board chose, after studying the scriptures, was to allow women to serve in leadership positions in the church.

Marcus, Reverend (Married), African American, Male: Marcus had an on-again-off-again relationship with church and God during his early years. He spent time in the military and is therefore receptive to female leadership. He believes women can be strong leaders and do an excellent job. He believes women have the same spiritual gifts as men and cannot understand the double standard toward women: "They can teach our male children but cannot teach men."

Michelle, Administrative Assistant and Elder (Single), African American, Female: Michelle grew up in a family church, but after going away to college, she turned away from God. It was during a really dark time in her life that she returned to the church. A group of women leaders helped her get back on track. She currently has a female pastor and has seen her church make great strides to expand its utilization of female leaders, but she admits it still has a long way to go. She is perplexed and grieved by the number of female churchgoers who do not support women in church leadership.

Antonio, Church Steward (Married), African American, Male: Antonio grew up in a Baptist church but now attends an African Methodist Episcopal Zion church. He believes women should be treated equally and believes it is the men's job to create a path for women to gain access to pastoral leadership. He also believes the church should be the example to the world in how we develop and encourage women to pursue senior-level church leadership positions.

Diane, Elder (Married), African American, Female: Diane grew up in the Baptist church and is an educator by vocation. She believes women are the creative center of the church and have the nurturing ability to meet the needs of church members. She also believes that women can do anything that God empowers them to do. She has seen women be poorly treated in the marketplace and in the church, but she is appalled that the church insists on using women to do the work of the church but won't grant them the authority to lead the church even though they are fully capable of doing so.

Judy, Program Pastor (Married), Caucasian, Female: Judy grew up in a Presbyterian church. She was the apple of her dad's eye, and he always nurtured her leadership qualities. She experienced intense isolation and criticism when she accepted an eldership position at her church. She believes without women in leadership, the church is lopsided and doesn't give full expression to the heart of God. Although she endeavors to remain hopeful that her church would make significant strides to expand the utilization of women, she knows of men and women who are steeped in patriarchal traditional thoughts that are unfair toward women.

"The Year of the Woman" was the societal mantra for 2019. Women were being celebrated and applauded for their historical political advancements in Congress. The #metoo movement, founded by Tarana Burke in 2006, was reinvigorated in 2018 as women found their voices and demanded change in the treatment of women in the marketplace. That resurgence was in an effort to put an end to ongoing sexual harassment and deplorable treatment of women seeking advancement or promotion in their respective fields.

While negative issues are constantly leaking out about male church leaders, the negative stories are not equally matched by stories heralding developments of women to positions of bishop, pastors, or elders. The church universal is eerily quiet in this regard. However, it won't be long before the critical conversation about the growing apathetic posture of men against women, and the visible growing absence of women in our churches, will draw both the stubborn and stuck men and women church vanguard to address these issues. I'm referring to those who despise the thought of women in church leadership. They will be confronted and forced to make drastic changes because the future success of the church will depend on it. A well-overdue paradigm shift in church culture is necessary. You, woman, the representative of Eve, are needed if the church is to survive. It may sound like a dramatic statement, but it's undeniably true.

Chapter 2

God's Purpose vs. Church Practice

The Struggle Between What I'm Competent to Do and What I'm Allowed to Do

*A*lthough we hear of women attaining success at various levels in arenas both in the marketplace and in ministry, there are still gigantic elephants in the rooms and halls of many churches: (1) gender discrimination, (2) blatant gender inequality, (3) gender oppression and bondage, and (4) chauvinistic platitudes. As women, we've done ourselves a huge disservice by dressing up the elephants, decorating the elephants, or justifying the elephants' existence so that we don't cause any trouble. What's worse, we may even know the elephants are there, but we won't call them what they are, and we'll dance around the issues. This makes me think of the women who feel they have to preach with a man's cadence, women believing they shouldn't cry or show "weak" emotions to demonstrate they can lead like a man, or women accepting salaries or honorariums when leading or speaking at churches that are less than their male counterparts.

I'm calling it exactly as I see it, and I am determined to address this formidable obstacle head on. These behaviors are being permitted to happen with the belief that men should have spiritual authority over women, whether qualified or not. Not only is this belief faulty—it's also dangerous. Since churches and church leaders refuse to address the issue of disparate treatment toward women, women have taken a severe blow to their sense of identity and self-esteem. The results show up in our inability to speak out against wrongdoing, to challenge behaviors and ideals that are contrary to Jesus's teachings, or to discover and hone our special God-given abilities when we are told, "You can't," "You won't," or "You're wrong." Somebody needs to call for answers and insist on constructive conversations to understand why we're not allowed full expression of our gifts or offered the freedom to develop programs or ministries that yet exist that will uplift women. Instead, women have been muted, ignored, and ostracized.

Again, the Bible makes it quite clear that God's daughters have the right to exist as equals to men even when laws and doctrines seem to contradict this notion. Numbers 27:1–11 recounts the case of Zelophehad's daughters. These were five sisters who had no brothers or uncles. When their father died, they presented their case to Moses and the elders of Israel, stating that even though they were women, they had a right to their father's inheritance. The law stipulated that only men could inherit property and currency. It was sacrilege and blasphemy for a woman to even think that she could dare be a beneficiary of her father's or husband's inheritance. But these five intelligent and courageous women were not about to let tradition and all four of the elephants mentioned earlier steal what they knew belonged to them. The women brought forth their case, and Moses prayed and asked God what the proper course of action should be. God clearly answered, "What Zelophehad's daughters are saying is right. You must certainly give them property as an inheritance among their father's relatives and give their father's inheritance to them" (Num. 27:7 NIV). God exploded the elephants in the room and yet again proved that he is against gender discrimination, blatant gender inequality, gender oppression and bondage, as well as chauvinistic platitudes.

Double Standards in Our Churches

When we as a society talk about women's empowerment and women's rights, we should not just hold accountable secular society for these freedoms; we must hold a magnifying glass up to our nation's churches to see what empowerment looks like for women from that perspective as well. Little girls who attend church grow up to be women. These women go out into the world, wanting to believe God's Holy Bible, which says that they are capable of having and accomplishing anything they are willing to work hard and have faith enough to achieve. If the words of the church don't match their actions, and women's education, experience, and prayers do not provide acceptance and opportunities for them within our churches, what are the levels of damage possible to female emotional, spiritual, and psychological well-being?

At the very least it is a double standard that cannot be scripturally supported, and at the very worst, we are crippling the church, the bride of Christ, from the full experiences of being uplifted, advanced in various spheres, and effective at the highest levels. Because of these slights toward women, the church is anemic and lacks any substantial power and influence. Can we call a spade a spade? If we continue to ignore the hypocrisy, the slights, the misinterpretation of scripture, and the poor selections of incompetent men over very capable and competent women, we are going to lose the vibrancy and perspective of exceptionally gifted women.

In my research study, men and women were asked specifically about their personal perspectives regarding women leaders' ability to effectively serve in church leadership. A person's level of competence and the belief that he/she has a calling to preach or lead in church were the most critical attributes for consideration. However, there existed a conflict between their *personal views* that women were just as capable of leading the church as they were of leading in the marketplace; and, their *church practices*, which demonstrated that women were treated as inadequate in leading the church and not afforded opportunities to prove otherwise.

The participants' responses were quite remarkable. The women participants in my study were unanimous in their belief that there was no difference between marketplace and church when selecting someone for a leadership position, yet many of them confided that they knew of other women who did not share the same sentiments. As for the men participants, some of them were challenged in reconciling their beliefs versus what was being permitted in their churches. The participants openly shared their views about women leaders. Let's look at some:

Bill: I know a few pastors who still remain rigid—a woman will not preach in this church.

Cornelius: I would not serve under a woman pastor, and that's just my personal preference.

Marcus: We still—we got certain positions that we'll put ladies in, or we think they should be in.

Antonio: I don't see a valid reason why any woman would not be able to step forward and just do what needs to be done in a church.

As you read these words, what are your immediate thoughts and feelings? In years past, I felt nothing. This way of treating women was so pervasive in the church that I didn't think anything of it. Additionally, if I'm honest, it simply wasn't my concern. I was only focused on fulfilling what I thought was God's purpose for *my* life. So I felt justified. I recently came to realize that I don't get to take a pass on this issue, and neither do you. As women, when we see unfair, unmerited, and unwarranted miscategorizations and mistreatment of women, we must be a voice for the voiceless until we help our sisters find their own voices. When we see this behavior, or hear these toxic viewpoints, we must be willing to challenge the status quo. This archaic thinking is no longer acceptable or beneficial to the church in any way. And since women make up the majority of churchgoers on a national scale, according to Pew Research,[1] it's time for a change, and we are the ones to bring it. As I listened to the men and women from my research study, the struggle for gender equality was the single most talked about issue, though it was discussed in varying degrees. Some shared that while women were qualified to do the work, men were still not willing to be pastored by them.

Pastors are not the only ones who still believe and teach patriarchal superiority. The debate amongst theologians and evangelical scholars about the role of women and God's intent for how they should function in the church, family, and society has not diminished. It has been centered on, for the most part, the scriptural interpretation of women. Gender-limiting information is still being taught in seminaries, where many of our men and women go to prepare for church leadership. While some biblical scholars believe that God created woman to be a "helper" to man in a subordinate capacity (according to Genesis 2), others think that the same scripture portrays women as a "helper" who is fully competent but with superior strength to establish oneness and *corulership* with man.[2] Consequently, there is great significance for the roles and identities of both male and female.[3] As we look at the current state of our churches, it would serve all involved to be more concerned with teaching what will bring stability, healing, unity, and posterity to the church. We must make a conscious effort to eradicate beliefs and teachings that divide, separate, harm, and neglect the women within our ranks who also have the responsibility and the God-given authority of caring for the church and its members.

Debated New Testament Scriptures

Let's do a little crash course in basic Theology 101 to show what this gender conflict is all about. Biblical doctrine is important and fundamental in Christianity. It is the basis for the teachings of Jesus Christ. Doctrine is the theological underpinnings or truths taught to support what occurred through the life and work of Jesus.[4] For every Christian believer, it is the Bible and Bible doctrine that is considered to be the trusted, infallible, authoritative word of God, though written by men.[5] The core tenants[6] of the Christian faith include the belief that:

- God does exist, and there is only one.
- God is all-powerful, God is all-knowing, and God is everywhere.
- God is love, God is holy, and God is righteous.
- God is a three-part being: Father, Jesus Christ the Son, and Holy Spirit.
- Jesus is God (fully God and fully man).
- Jesus was perfect and without sin.
- The Holy Spirit is God.
- The Bible is the "inspired" or "God-breathed" word of God.
- God's plan of salvation is a free gift to anyone who believes in Jesus.
- God created humans in the image of God.
- Death came into the world through Adam's sin.
- Sin separates us from God.

As you review these tenants, what is not included in Christian doctrine, however, is the issue of gender or the role of women as it relates to being Christian.

I believe it is safe to posit that biblical scholars', and Christian leadership's scriptural arguments against women pastoring a church; being a bishop in a church; being a deacon in a church; or holding any senior office in the church—especially where authority over male members is inescapable—are rooted mainly in Pauline New Testament scriptures. Now this hypothesis precludes the power-hungry, sexist gender discrimination that runs rampant in both religious and secular settings at large. That ilk has a set agenda that has nothing to do with righteousness and godliness. The scholars and leaders I will be referring to in this book are Christians who staunchly accept as true that God, according to holy scripture, disqualifies women from major leadership positions in the church regardless of credentials or the woman's belief that she has been called by God.

The table below lists the Bible verses male leadership often uses to make their argument against female leadership.

Debated New Testament Scriptures

Bible Chapter and Verses	Themes Relating to Women	Scriptural Text
1 Corinthians 14:34–35 (NKJV)	Women Remain Silent in Church	Let your women keep silent in the churches, for they are not permitted to speak; but they are to be submissive, as the law also says. And if they want to learn something, let them ask their own husbands at home; for it is shameful for women to speak in church.
1 Timothy 2:11–12 (NKJV)	Women Not Permitted to Teach a Man	Let a woman learn in silence with all submission. And I do not permit a woman to teach or to have authority over a man, but to be in silence.
1 Timothy 3:2, 12 (NKJV)	Qualifications of a Bishop and a Deacon	A bishop then must be blameless, the husband of one wife, temperate, sober-minded, of good behavior, hospitable, able to teach ... Let deacons be the husbands of one wife, ruling their children and their own houses well.
Ephesians 5:22–24 (NKJV)	Wives Submit to Husbands	Wives, submit to your own husbands, as to the Lord. For the husband is head of the wife, as also Christ is head of the church; and He is the Savior of the body. Therefore, just as the church is subject to Christ, so let the wives be to their own husbands in everything.

In no way can the adherence to or the refuting of these scriptures add to or take away from anyone's ability to be a follower of Jesus. Nonetheless, the continued conflict about them lives on, knowing that it is indisputable that arguments can be made for and against each scripture to support or deny the right of women to lead and teach in the church.

These scriptures, when not properly interpreted, provide the backdrop on which centuries of discrimination against women in the church have been cultivated and doctrinalized. Interpretation is certainly key when using biblical passages to exclude an entire gender from ever claiming a call via the fivefold ministry gifts as defined in Ephesians 4:11–12 (NKJV):

> And he gave some, apostles; and some, prophets; and some, evangelists; and some, pastors and teachers; For the perfecting of the saints, for the work of the ministry, for the edifying of the body of Christ.

Now, based on a *literal* interpretation of the offending, antiwomen in leadership scriptures listed in the table above, what people believe Paul really meant in his epistle to the Ephesians in 4:11–12 was:

> And he gave some, *male* apostles; and some, *male* prophets; and some, *male*, evangelists (but sometimes women); and some, *male* pastors; and *male* teachers (but sometimes women teachers if they do not have any *male* students); Because only *males* (for the most part) can be used by God for the perfecting of the saints, for the work of the ministry, for the edifying of the body of Christ.

Think carefully before dismissing my rewording of Ephesians 4:11–12 as it relates to the table scriptures, as exaggerated. If women must keep silent in the church, and must only be taught at home by their husbands (God forbid if they are not married), then that makes it absolutely impossible for them to ever be a part of the fivefold ministry.

The Old Testament is filled with women leaders. Deborah was a judge over Israel and a warrior who fought side by side with men (Judges 4–5). Miriam, Moses's older sister, was a prophet, a leader, and a spokesperson during Israel's exodus. Don't forget Huldah, the prophetess, whose insight and wisdom about the nation was sought over that of Jeremiah. She was the popular prophet of that day (2 Kings 22:14–20; 2 Chronicles 34:22–33).

God is most certainly progressive, and to believe that he would regress women from the powerful roles they played in the Old Testament before his son even redeemed humankind, to making them mere pawns today who quietly submit to the will of every man in the church, is completely out of God's character. When does God ever go backward? What could possibly motivate him to retard his thinking about the role that women should play in the earth, and especially in his newly formed church?

First Timothy 2:11–12 says that a woman must keep silent in the church with all submission and that a woman cannot teach a man or have authority over a man. This verse is heavily quoted when addressing the issue of why women cannot be pastors and leaders in the church. Yet the very genesis of the New Testament church refers to actual house churches (which existed way before the first church building was erected) that were headed by women. In Acts 12:12 the house of Mary, John Mark's mother (John Mark being the author of the book of Mark), was a place where Christians went to pray. The passage overtly says that the apostle Peter, once released from prison by an angel, went to Mary's house to let the saints know that he had been released from prison miraculously. Why would Peter go to this woman's house unless he knew that Christians would already be gathered there? Surely Mary held "church" meetings at her house regularly, and I doubt seriously if she turned over her manor to someone else's authority because he was male.

Aquila and Pricilla pastored a church in their home (1 Corinthians 16:19). Yes, this is a husband and wife team, but Pricilla is still a designated pastor and leader, and all of the Christian churches at the time seemed to be just fine with her role.

Colossians 4:15 mentions the church that is in Nympha's home. If this woman was not the pastor of the church, why didn't Paul just send greetings to the pastor and thank Nympha for the use of her house? No, he sent a greeting to Nympha herself, indicating that she was the head of the operation.

Our modern sensibilities and male-centric way of viewing the church obscures the undiluted love, compassion, and perfectly practical way the early church operated without respect of persons, persuasions, wealth, or gender. God has made it very clear in his scriptures that his family can be used however he sees fit, and he sees fit to pour out his Spirit on *all* flesh.

> In the last days, God says, I will pour out my Spirit on all people. Your sons and daughters will prophesy, your young men will see visions, your old men will dream dreams. Even on my servants, both men and women, I will pour out my Spirit in those days, and they will prophesy. (Acts 2:17–18 NIV)

The Dominant Male Perspective

The monetization of Christianity and the church at large has caused the barking dogs to ravish the church because of its tremendous earning power and its potential to control and manipulate the masses. Jesus dealt with this "money changers" attitude in Matthew 21:12 when he ran out the merchandizers who thought it was perfectly fine for them to peddle their wares for convenience to the people of God who needed doves and such for their offerings. He fashioned a whip and overturned tables to let everyone know that he meant business about them not turning his Father's house into a den of thieves. Look at how far things had gone from Moses's instructions to the people on how to worship God—to merchants fleecing the sheep with the blessing of the organized religious leaders—who surely got their cut of the profits. This same "fleecing" mindset is one of the brass tactics erected today in the struggle to silence and control women in the church. But this time they're fleecing our money *and* our authority. By misinterpreting scripture, and dogmatically declaring that a man's God-given right is to have all women submit to him, while she can never hold a position of leadership, makes the commission of God sound more like a lopsided screenplay from a 1980s sexploitation film than a desire to see the church operating at its full capacity in the world. God has made it clear that a major part of our victory on the earth is in our unity with each other, and by following that agenda, we will see his will done on the earth.

> For as many of you as were baptized into Christ have put on Christ. There is neither Jew nor Greek, there is neither slave nor free, there is neither male nor female; for you are all one in Christ Jesus. (Galatians 3:27–28 NKJV)

Just to test the use of these scriptures as antiwoman fodder within the Christian church, I posed this question to my research participants to better understand what they had been taught from the scriptures to justify their stance on the role of women. Here's what some of them shared:

> **Suzanne:** In church—church at large, not my church, but in church—there's still people who don't believe that women should pastor because they take that one little 1 Corinthians scripture that says that women should be at home teaching their children, but forget to look at the whole context of that teaching.

> **Anna:** The mindset of a lot of men is they cannot sit under a woman pastor because of some writings that Paul did in the book of Corinthians and I think in the book of Timothy where he addressed women in leadership authority.

> **Michelle:** Now, I don't know whether they held the leadership positions in that church, but you know, another pastor spoke of how it is, ... some of the women who are like, "I don't want a female pastor." Which I can't understand. You know, I can't even

wrap my mind around that. I'm like what would make you say that. I just think it's, if anything, ignorance. You know? Because you have that, you know, people take Paul out of context when he said, "Let the women be silent." Not understanding he was specifically writing to an issue that was pertaining to that church at that time, but not that he was shunning women from the ministry.

Diane: They go back to where it was in 1 Timothy where women were to be silent. Women were to be silent you know; women were to know their place. And of course, I've learned since then how that scripture has been misinterpreted.

The dominant male perspective is not only used in deciding the fate of women based on nondoctrinal scriptures, but many denominations also subscribe to four generally accepted perspectives about women to categorize a woman's right to function within the church:[7] (1) the *traditional or complementary view* is that women should not be involved in ministry; (2) the *male leadership view* is that women could be included in ministry only if they are under the covering of a man; (3) the *plural ministry view* is that both men and women are ministers, yet the overemphasis of ordination has caused the narrowing perspective of women and, (4) the *egalitarian view* is that men and women are equal concerning all things related to church and ministry and God calls them both.

Now that we've looked at this issue from a theological viewpoint, let's also look at statistical data that reveals what women are saying about this patriarchal mindset. Barna Research Group[8] surveyed over 608 female churchgoers across the United States and found that 78 percent of women disagreed with the statement that the Bible prohibits women from holding leadership positions within the church, and 37 percent of those women believed that ministries would be more effective if more women were given the opportunity to lead. It's sad to think that women are being oppressed and treated like second-class citizens in the church.

Many of the male participants in my research unabashedly admitted that they have known and currently know very talented women who are knowledgeable and excellent leaders, yet, they are not given equal consideration to pastor churches even though they work hard, have an education, and believe they are called by God to preach and teach the scriptures. Instead of ordinations and leadership opportunities being determined based on good character, trustworthiness, competence, skills, abilities, and proven experience, leadership choices are made primarily by the sheer fact that a person has a vagina or a penis, and it's dictating who can teach and lead people. What a shame and a disgrace.

Chapter 3

Men vs. Women

If We're Both Wearing Our Armor,
Who Can Tell Us Apart?

*W*hile in the military, I trained alongside my fellow male comrades. At no time during our military exercises did we compete with one another. Everyone was assigned a specific task and needed to focus on performing their tasks well so the entire unit would pass on to the next level. We supported one another and protected one another, knowing the final outcome of the exercise always depended upon our ability to work as a unit. During different types of trainings, whether physically rigorous or classroom instruction, I had the honor and experience of leading both men and women who were serving in the navy or marines. Whenever I was selected to lead, it was solely because I had earned the right to lead. These selections were made objectively by my superiors, who were sometimes men and at other times women. Gender was never part of the decision-making process.

As young military personnel, we were taught early to respect those in uniform. We were all skilled in our specific areas of expertise, and we depended upon one another to do our jobs well. To serve in the military, gender only came into play based on the type of occupation chosen, but so did, height, weight, and age. In positions where both men and women were accepted and qualified, gender never determined who was selected for leadership. Men and women were selected based on ability (and that did not necessarily mean physical strength).

When men and women choose to take a sworn oath to serve our country, they recognize that they share the same enemies, which means they are on the same team. Servicemen and servicewomen are admonished to protect one another, no matter what. This concept of protection is drilled into anyone joining the armed forces. Once I joined the military, I became the property of the US government. And once I put on that uniform, my identity merged with the others who were part of the naval command. Throughout the military, no matter which branch, men and women become one body recognized as the armed services, and their number-one priority and responsibility is to protect the United States of America and her interests. That's the culture and the standard that we accept and abide by.

As another powerful example of organizational unity, we see this commitment to a mission, without respect for gender, being demonstrated and applauded by the National Aeronautics and Space Administration (NASA). Most recently we've witnessed the very first all-female astronaut spacewalk team in space. Jessica Meir and Christina Koch made history with a feat that has never been accomplished. Although women have joined space teams in the past, having only women, with no male presence onboard the spacecraft, is unprecedented. According to NASA,[1] the all-female team was not purposefully planned. However, they stated that it was an inevitability since the 2013 graduating astronaut class that these two women belonged to was made up of 50 percent women—the highest it's ever been.

These women astronauts believe it is necessary for young girls to see what is possible for them to accomplish, and the women astronauts highlighted the importance of sharing their experiences and their stories to help build interest and support for anyone who aspires to a career in the aeronautical field. These women have been educated, trained, and prepared to serve the United States in this monumental way, and it's heralded as history making by the rest of us who are watching in awe. These women astronauts share a goal of making a contribution to the field of science along with their male astronaut comrades, and they pursued that dream without considering that their gender might impede such a desire. While this is plausible, this should not be extraordinary. It should be the norm. And based on these women and the others who work alongside them for this common goal, it's just a matter of time before women astronaut teams will be commonplace.

Gender Discrimination Against Women

The strides being made in our society keep failing to grace the pulpits of America's churches in a noteworthy way. For some reason, the church, established as a patriarchal institution, has yet to learn the power of unity and respect for every member as an elite force, recognized as the body of Christ. We might prove to be more effective in accomplishing God's plan to advance his kingdom here on earth if we took the limits off and removed the barriers of entry to clergywomen. Instead, the church uses gendered criteria to determine what roles, responsibilities, opportunities, and structures will be put in place as the dictate for interaction and operation, technically called gender framing.[2]

So basically, this means when people in the church see that you're either a man or a woman, that awareness will determine how they will treat you, what you will have access to, what rules will be applicable to you, how relevant your voice and ideas will be to the goals of the church, and whether or not you will be afforded consideration for high-level leadership appointments. It blows my mind that gender framing is still an issue in the twenty-first century. Men leaders in the church continue ignoring or marginalizing the tremendous exploits achieved by women clergy, and instead, their gender is what is considered first. When deciding to connect with a church, as a woman, your gender is what will determine what will be available to you. Your gender will either reward you or penalize you. Gender carries with it advantages and disadvantages, limitations and barriers, stereotypes and prejudices.

Why have we, the men and women who are opposed to this mistreatment, not questioned, challenged, or called a halt to this foolishness when we've encountered it? It is irrefutable that women are strong and powerful, yet for some reason, we acquiesce to being treated disrespectfully by our spiritual leaders, whether it's intentional or unintentional. This gendered cultural acceptance of blatant discrimination is the culprit for the ill effects this mindset is having overall on our churches. One way or another, the Christian church will be required to respond to a growing demand for change against gender discrimination.

The unhealthy status of the church is proof that our current methods for dealing with gender discrimination are not working. Based on my research, the gender discrimination issue was not really championed by the women within the churches selected. Surprisingly, the issue was raised mostly by the men. Also important to note is that the gender issue was never raised in response to women's attempts to be powerful. It arose from women's attempts to not be rejected and discounted. Statistics show that most women don't see themselves as leaders even when they are in positions of influence. Mainly, they see themselves as servants.[3] Many of the participants in my study shared experiences related to this notion of gender framing:

> **Yvette:** They [church leadership] did put some women at the table, but they didn't have a title. So they were there ... and you sat in with the elders, but you didn't have any—not voting privileges. You weren't going to speak on a level where it made a decision. So you could—you may have influenced the decision, but you didn't have a final say in the decision.

> **Antonio:** He [his friend] was like, "Oh, there's no way that a woman can be the pastor of a church. It's like, how is that even possible?" I'm like, what makes you think the way that women are would make them not be able to do leadership in a church? And his response was, no, because they have a family, and they have kids, and other responsibilities. And I'm like, well, don't you have family, and don't you

have kids? So does that mean that you can't do leadership in the church? And he's like, "No, but women are different."

Judy: I think overall in the church we are well behind the marketplace. Well behind. And I think it all depends on the denomination. I know that in evangelical Christianity I would say we are well behind. ... valuing women as fully equal partners in ministry... I think women in the marketplace have much more opportunity probably because they're not living in that old, old biblical mentality.

Anna: We have a couple of presiding elders that are females. Well, these are very powerful women. But one of the things that we struggle with, even in [church name], we are women. For example, we cannot wear open-toed shoes in the pulpit because men have [foot] fetishes. We cannot wear earrings, big earrings, in the pulpit. Or when we're at the annual conference and we are in procession, we have had men that come down looking at our ears. I think a lot of that is going away. I think the open-toe shoes are going away. But I think a lot of the earrings—I think we've resolved that. But here, again, it's not looking at us as pastors or preachers. It's looking at us as female pastors.

Bill: Seminary liberated me. And it was done simplistically. Prior to going to seminary, what fortified my understanding of women not being in ministry was that when I heard a woman preach, she sounded like a man, and I knew that wasn't right. Okay. You're a woman. How are you going to sound like a man? And so that was a complete turnoff for me, and it validated for me what my pastor told me.

In a nation where we encourage freedom of speech, it seems the church chooses to continue to subjugate women based on archaic beliefs that are not culturally pertinent. Our bodies are demonized and used as weapons against us. Our character, our intentions, and our mannerisms are subject to scrutiny for baseless reasons. If we're too smart, too direct, ask too many questions, speak up too much, are too beautiful, are not beautiful enough, are too shapely, are too manly, are too plain, or dare to be ambitious, especially in the church, these are all reasons men use to reject us and reject our gifts. Let's face it, men are hindered by gender framing. In the same way that no one wants to be denied rights based on race, how dare we uphold a justification to suppress the advancement of women in any way. To be dehumanized or silenced goes against the fabric of who we are as human beings, and when this occurs, it will cause an individual to either fight or shrink back. What we are seeing in the earth today is Eve emerging. Women are waking up, gaining their strength, getting their footing, finding their voices, and determining that enough is enough!

Women Are Valuable

As valuable as women are to the viability of the church, our contributions are stymied because of who God physically made us to be. The misogynistic way many men speak of women who preach would make one think that *that* woman has committed some heinous crime. These types of men specifically disdain the thought of women in positions of authority over them and it is most obvious in churches. This behavior should be discouraged, and anyone spewing such hatred should be removed. It's not productive, it's not loving, and it's ungodly to treat someone with higher regard than you would someone else based on their physicality or status in the community (Romans 2:11). Jesus gave us beautiful examples of how he interacted with women and how he utilized women, all in ways that were contrary to the culture of the day.

Even in churches where the leaders embrace an egalitarian view (upholding that men and women are equal), there are stories of churches that have split or have become severely divided when women have been allowed to hold leadership positions. What we fail to assess and correct is the impact of this type of rejection toward women. I can't stress enough that it is a blow to a woman's sense of self, and she inevitably will struggle with accepting who she is. Anyone or any organization that is responsible for causing this kind of pain has become devoid of awareness relating to the consequences of their actions. God help us.

It is in conditions like these that we women must remember that we are made in the likeness and image of God and that our external and internal frameworks have unapologetically been designed for a specific purpose. The Bible teaches in Genesis that Eve was fashioned from the rib of Adam. According to the scriptures, God determined that women are a suitable companion for men. That means we are equal and complementary to men in every way, including leadership. Being a complement doesn't exclude women from church leadership. A woman may be a different kind of leader (based on temperament, style, focus). She may lead in different areas (pastoral, elder, prophet, teacher, bishop) but be a leader nonetheless—not subservient or less than a man.

So what does this all mean? This means it is *your* job to understand this truth and fully embrace and explore what God had in mind when he created you to represent him in the earth as a woman. You do not need a man to validate what God has already established for you. Anytime you encounter anyone who refuses to recognize your value, it is *your* responsibility to remove yourself from such negative environments and find connections with people that align with your beliefs about who God has made you to be. It is not a woman's job to convince others of her worth. Let God fight those battles. It *is* her job, however, to live a blameless life, which is the same responsibility required of men.

It is this very callous and unfair treatment of women that sparked the women's suffragist and later the feminist movement. Suffragists fought for the right of women's voices to be heard at the ballot box. The general idea of feminism is that women should be treated similarly as men in all areas of opportunity, to include civil and social rights, as well as being given equal respect at home, on the job, and at church.[4] As women began to successfully campaign for their rights in the late nineteenth century, additional questions emerged about women's function within the home and the church, causing a deeper rift within society. These questions also sparked debates regarding a woman's "place" in the family, the church, and her relationship with God.[5]

Feminism

Although feminism has had a reputation of taking gender equity and equality to the extreme, many Christian women differ in their opinions about the degree to which women are leading in the church. They fully embrace gender roles and do not subscribe to the need to eradicate or be redefined by them. I agree with this sentiment. While I am a staunch supporter of gender equality, as a wife and mother of two adult sons, I clearly see why God decreed for men and women to occupy this earth and reign together. I don't believe our strengths and abilities are predicated on our gender. This sentiment may be hard for some to accept.

In our home, my husband and I have different functions, but we're both capable of leading. Our strengths and abilities dictate who should be in charge of the finances, who should be in charge of cooking, who should be in charge of helping with homework, or who should repair broken things. These decisions are not automatically based on gender. This is a blessing not a curse! I want to make that clear. My husband and I parent our children understanding that they need different things at different junctures of their lives, and we have to determine which parent will do what part to make sure our sons get what they need. We didn't always feel this way and were raised differently, but as a new couple, starting a new family, we had to figure out what would work best for us and be willing to change, grow, and release old paradigms if we wanted our marriage and family to thrive based on our needs and desires.

As a stay-at-home mom during our sons' formative years, I worked on nurturing their sense of self, serving others, character development, learning to be appreciative and showing gratitude, and establishing a sense of responsibility and teamwork by being assigned chores and playing sports. During that time, my husband supported and reinforced what I was teaching. My social work education and background was a critical component for our partnering way of parenting. When our sons were younger, I primarily drove them to school and picked them up. Once they reached middle school, my husband took this role. During this critical time of development, my husband took more of the lead role for the children by helping them establish their sense of identity, become critical thinkers, develop their goals and aspirations for the future, implement a strong work ethic, and create daily schedules. He was also teaching them how to address peer pressure and become competitive in every area of life.

This partner parenting technique we used served our sons well in the classroom, in their social environments, and in their athletic endeavors. I in turn supported and reinforced my husband's efforts in these areas. Our sons knew that my husband and I were working together and could not be pitted against one another to get whatever they wanted. Since my husband and I both knew what the other was working on, we could easily step in if the other had to be away or was occupied with something else. We chose to work together at every developmental stage, and there was no such thing as a woman's role or a man's job. This also applied to cooking, cleaning, and disciplining. The job was called parenting or running the household. Whatever we were doing, we did it together. We learned to serve one another and to submit to one another for the common good of the whole. This same concept can be applied anywhere, but it's a mindset, and it's a choice.

In our Western culture, we subscribe to a gendered way of thinking about men and women's roles in the home that is now dramatically evolving. The traditional thoughts about husbands and wives is no longer feasible since the income of both the man and the woman, the interests of both the man and the woman, and the abilities of both the man and the woman are factors to be considered. Neither spouse should be demanding anything of the other when both are needed for the sustainability of the family's financial well-being. US Department of Labor statistics (2019) show that 57.1 percent of women are in the workforce and 77.6 percent of mothers work outside of the home.[6]

This reality is becoming ever clearer in our career choices as well. Although we still see propensities for discrepancies in the earning potential of men and women, this has more to do with career field interests than ability.[7] It's not that women aren't smart enough to do certain types of jobs, like being a pilot, an architect, a computer programmer, or law enforcement; they just prefer to work in other areas. However, when a woman does decide she wants to pursue careers in these areas, including as a clergy member,[8] under no circumstance should they be discouraged, or worse, restricted from doing so.

When it comes to mainstream feminism, studies suggest that being identified as a feminist has been especially challenging for Christian women. We often struggle with deciding if we are willing to be identified as such or rather to strictly tout our beliefs in equality and liberation theology, which emphasizes freedom from social, political, and economic oppression. It's an intense debate even to the degree that some Christian circles consider upholding a feminism banner as being akin to using a curse word that may be taken by some as an offense.[9] This challenge is exponentially greater for African American women when considering the intersectionality of gender, race, and ability, among other things that make this issue even harder to confront and overcome. In the next chapter, we'll look at some organizations that teeter on both sides of this gender debate.

The Battle of the Sexes Continues

Because of the constant ridicule and criticism about gender and how women should act, what we can do, and whether or not we should be permitted to fulfill leadership callings, women also struggle with what it even means to be feminine as a leader. In another research study that sought to understand gender dynamics and why women are still battling acceptance in the church, it was discovered that while the majority of women want to see major changes made in the church in this area of gender equality, men do not.[10] This creates a battle of the sexes mentality. In this scenario, we aren't realizing that while we're competing and pitting men against women soldiers, who are all in the army of the Lord, the church is dying, causing everyone to lose.

In the research study I conducted, the women participants shared that they felt they must exude patience and understanding instead of directly and immediately addressing wrongdoing or double standards against women in the church. Some participants classified the bias against women as not being able to penetrate the "good old boy network" where the men leaders look out for one another and select friends for leadership positions instead of considering who is the most qualified or best fit for the role. Another argument the participants made was that they believe it's important to maintain a gender balance in an environment where the majority of the churchgoers are women. Still others argued that it should not be about gender, but about calling, destiny, gifts, abilities, and passion, all wrapped up in the package of a person. Sadly, these perspectives still fuel an ongoing debate.

When God created Eve, he looked upon her and was satisfied with his handiwork. I want to encourage all women by saying that God's approval of us has not changed. In fact, he's waiting on each one of us to do exactly what he created us to do. Your job is to discover what that is, prepare yourself to be great at your craft, and then go out there and make a difference. To become a leader for the kingdom of God doesn't begin with an ordination or recognition within the church building.

To successfully adopt this way of thinking requires a kingdom mindset with the ability to see the world as your ministry field. This is in direct contrast to a church mindset, where women might narrowly focus on what's happening in the organized church buildings where we worship. We are sanctioned by God to be his ambassadors. His armor (Ephesians 6:10-18) has already been provided for us to function, so put it on! Add good character traits such as integrity, compassion, and a servant's heart and we are ready to go. In God's eyes, when women equip themselves with the attributes that *he* deems to be important, we become Christ-like, and he's prone to assign us to do anything, anywhere! No gender distinction required. He's already made us soldiers fit for his purposes. At that point, there is nothing left for us to prove.

Chapter 4

Women vs. Women

Sabotage, Silence, or Support—Is Your Stance
Hindering or Helping Other Women?

Sabotage

*W*e may be our own worst critics, but other women are certainly our worst enemies. In chapter 3, what I didn't tell you about my military experience is before I left for bootcamp at the tender age of eighteen, I remember being a visitor at a friend's Baptist church weeks prior. My friend introduced me to a few of the members, telling them that I was getting ready to go into the military. An elderly African American woman I didn't know came over to speak with me. After asking me a few questions about me joining the military, she suggested that I must be a promiscuous woman or "loose" if I was going into the military because ladies don't join the military. Yep, that's right. You might want to read that again. Her actual choice of words were not as nice as I'm describing them. I was stunned, confused, and in utter disbelief by her ignorant remarks. I began defending myself and explained the amazing opportunity the military would be for me to travel and get an education. My justification fell on deaf ears.

Her judgment of me was already cemented. Once she left me, I stood there in shock at what had just transpired. When I told my friend what happened, she rolled her eyes and told me to ignore the old woman.

I didn't understand the negative connection the elderly woman was making between me being a female and my decision to join the military. I couldn't understand why my being a female would matter. As a young woman, I hadn't been brainwashed yet about my gendered boundaries. As I think back on it, she was trying to limit me and create doubt in me. In essence, she was nonchalantly sabotaging the excitement I had around my own goals and choices. This woman didn't know me and had never seen me before in her life. Yet, she felt comfortable speaking harshly over me. She didn't know my personal (and financial) reasons for joining the service, and she didn't care. All she knew was that in her mind, I was a girl. I should not pursue the military.

Since I knew she didn't know me, her words weren't taken to heart, but they did sting. As you can see, I've never forgotten what she said. I am sharing this so that women can take the same posture with anyone who is telling them what they cannot or should not do. It is critical that you ignore people like that—and then dismiss them. Sometimes it's easier said than done, but it is imperative that as you are discovering who you are and where you are going, that you only surround yourself with people who can encourage and support you. This may require that you leave family, friends, relationships, and yes, even churches.

While that experience was over thirty years ago, my research participants shared more recent stories about experiences with women that are just as grievous. Two of the women participants, Yvette and Judy, who attended the nondenominational church that chose to open up their elders' board to include women, shared negative experiences they had with other women when the news was announced that they were going to be added to the all-male elders' board.

> **Yvette:** I was walking out of church one Sunday, and okay, so it was three of us—yeah it was three of us—three of us [up] on the screen [being ordained

as elders]. And one of the elder candidates died. She
died before we were commissioned. And so that was
really, really difficult, and she was one of the ones
who in the beginning had been sitting at the table.
She was an older lady. She had a lot of wisdom. So
finally, she was being able to see the culmination,
but she didn't make it to be commissioned. So when
she died, I'm walking out of church one Sunday
and this lady says to me, "Well you know that's
because you're not in God's will and so which one of
you all is going to be next?" So she's going out and
I'm coming in and I'm sitting in the sanctuary and
somebody had come up to just congratulate me, you
know, the mature people they come up and so I just
casually mentioned, I said, "You know somebody
just said to me, which one of you all is going to
die next, me or Judy." And so, she immediately
recognized it as a curse that this woman had put
on me. And she said—she grabbed me, and I didn't
know what was happening, and we went back to
this room, and she called some other people. She
says, "Come on, we're going to pray!" And she says,
"We don't accept curses." I'd never been a part of
anything like that. I never took it as a curse, but
she spiritually recognized that she was pronouncing
a curse over us.

Yvette and Judy agonized over their decision to accept this
new leadership role primarily because their family upbringing and
church culture told them that women were not supposed to lead
in this way. When they decided to say yes and take the eldership
position, it was after weeks of prayer and seeking guidance from
family, spouses, and Bible reading. These women were fearful and
uncertain, yet something inside of them felt watered and validated
when they were offered such responsibility. Something that was
dormant came alive inside of them, and they trusted that God
knew better.

It breaks my heart to hear women speak of their freedom in

terms of bondage. Even though we live in a country where we can aspire to anything we desire to accomplish, there are these little pockets of society, whether it be a family, a church, or a company, where mental and emotional enslavement and limitations still hinder a woman's forward advancement. It starts with negative words spoken. The words take root in our hearts and minds, and then they become a belief that we erroneously embody.

> **Judy:** It's interesting. When we made the decision [to become elders], it was more strong women that had the issue than men. I got more emails from strong women that I would have thought, "Yeah, finally!" But they weren't. I cried a lot. And there was a lot of self-doubt, there was a lot of, "Did I not hear? Did we not hear God correctly?" Like, "What if we're not being obedient?" I think the [question] that lingered probably my whole tenure of being an elder is, "Am I being obedient or am I just doing what I want to do?" Or you know, doing what they say I should do. Deep down I knew this was the best thing for our church, not just me but women. I didn't care who the women were actually [who had the issue], and yet I had that little lingering doubt, self-doubt.

It seems that women may make demeaning and sabotaging statements about other women without any consideration that their thoughts and words will potentially impact the female target as either a unique brand of *judgment* or misguided *protection*. Women who judge so carelessly lack understanding about that woman's personal dreams, desires, necessities, or sense of calling. When a woman becomes an object for misjudgment instead of a person to be encouraged, we lose sight of how our actions impede our sister's development and sense of identity. When women feel obligated to "protect" another woman from committing "sin" for being "out of order," they do not realize that they themselves are victims of male-dominated brainwashing. Yes, such women have bought the lie that women are not equally empowered to serve

God in functions that are equal to those of men. These protective women honestly believe they are helping keep women from being tricked by the devil or operating with a Jezebel spirit by being too assertive, confident, or outspoken. Facebook is riddled with such feminine crusaders of all ages who bash and chastise women for believing they are "allowed" to preach or hold leadership positions in the church! Their language is filled with venom and hatred. It is sad because the ridicule is misguided and anti-Christ behavior.

Words are powerful enough to uplift or tear down. Women cannot be so trite about things they don't understand or agree with. We all have a responsibility to be mindful of our words. If the leadership action a woman is taking is not illegal or immoral, give your sister the benefit of the doubt. At the very least pray for her. We should always strive to be a force for good and not evil toward one another.

Silence

Perhaps you've never sabotaged another woman. Instead you've done nothing. The dangerous thing about silence is that it can be construed as complicity. To be complicit means you are helping to commit a wrongdoing. Inaction is still an action. There is a famous quote, "The only thing necessary for the triumph of evil is for good men to do nothing."[1] When we watch another woman being discriminated against, oppressed, treated unfairly, marginalized, ridiculed, ostracized, belittled, used, silenced, or any other degrading act that demonstrates opposition to her advancement as a woman, we are helping to demoralize her. That's a hard pill to swallow!

If we see something, we must be courageous enough to say something. "See something, say something" is a mantra for all public spaces in America. As a society, we are agreeing to help law enforcement keep us safe by reporting any misconduct we see in stores, on planes, on trains, or in any public places. We should extend this same support to our sisters. As women, we need to uphold this mantra in the church as well. If you see something, say something.

As we consider this request to self-police in our churches, there is information you need to know about what you're up against. The patriarchal church institution and cultural norms that have been accepted by both men and women breed an environment that keeps women stuck. Because women are active and busy in church, it may not always be easy to spot misconduct, and what's worse, some may believe or accept that such behavior is appropriate against women. It's not. So when something inappropriate is occurring, be willing to promptly alert someone in senior leadership who is responsible to address your concerns. If that doesn't work, you will have to determine if you're willing to be in an environment where such conduct is overlooked or condoned.

Sadly, however, many church attenders believe the plight of women cannot and will not change. One study revealed that less than one percent supported a woman in the role of pastor.[2] This rationale is commonly attributed to traditions, church doctrine, and theology.[3] One might think with this degree of pushback by both men and women, women would simply find something else to do with their lives, but they don't. As church leaders, they press forward and just deal with the disrespect. Who in their right mind would choose this? It stands to reason that there is something or someone greater than themselves that compels women to continue down the path of becoming clergy. These issues that women clergy deal with are widespread denominationally. The role of women in the Baptist church has been a source of contention for decades. Seventh-Day Adventist, Lutheran, Church of God in Christ, Episcopal, Methodist, Presbyterian, United Methodist, Mennonite, United Church of Christ, and nondenominational churches share the same challenges with women pastors, Protestant and Pentecostal churches alike.

From some of the data I gathered, researchers reported experiences of women pastors who attended these various denominations. For those of us who don't believe in women pastors; who have not taken the time to understand the stories of women pastors; or who have not considered the resistance or personal sacrifices of women pastors, here are some of the issues they've faced along with the coping mechanisms these women have employed to survive:[4]

Issues

- Constantly second-guessing themselves, wondering if they made the right decision by being a pastor
- Wrestling with thoughts of discounting their callings to pastor
- Constant hardships, isolation, judgment, ridicule, and conflict with other church leaders and churchgoers
- Being told what preaching style women should have and how to fulfill other clergy duties based on the expectations of others
- Tempted to maintain traditional or religious standards or norms for women to keep the peace
- Personal feelings of a sense of obligation to challenge patriarchy in the church and society and to point out gender bias
- Feeling obligated to support and address women's rights issues (without coming across as a feminist)
- Confronted with ongoing prejudice that would be considered discrimination in other work environments
- Challenged with how to address church problems if their leadership style isn't considered feminine enough
- Balancing the traditional family values that highlight the patriarchal model for both home and church

Coping Mechanisms

- Prayer to manage the pain from not being accepted
- Speaking directly to those in opposition to their position and addressing the issue
- Ignoring the gender issues
- Pretending not to be affected by the negativity to remain effective as a pastor

The theme of women resisting women was quite pronounced in my research findings. As participants discussed this topic, it appeared to surprise both the men and the women to what extent the resistance existed of women against other women.

Marcus: And I feel that—not just men. There are some ladies out there who feel that they shouldn't have a woman leader!

Anna: You will hear women today—a lot of women today don't think that women—a woman is ready to lead this country. Not just males. Women! They think leadership is associated with males.

Generational differences also played a significant part in perceptions of women that were shared by the research participants. Older women were described as more likely to resist and reject women as leaders than younger women.

Cornelius: The older saints are hesitant and reluctant because they again are used to the old paradigm, and even to this day they welcome the male presence more than they do the female presence.

Diane: Well, I think not so much among the younger generation, but I think among women in my generation. I think there are some of us who still can't embrace the idea of women being that active in ministry ... and some of it has to do also with the dynamics that goes on between women in church: jealousy, envy, whatever is there.

At the same time, others recognized the value of women leaders and spoke of the influence women have had on them specifically.

James: I think it's fantastic. So, like I would see somebody like [name], who is someone that I feel led by oftentimes. You know, we're, we [are both leaders] in different settings, but she's changed my life. She's a remarkable, godly, wise woman of God ... her being a woman is not an issue to me.

Suzanne: So when you have women who can appreciate what each of them have to offer, then you can develop a real good team of leadership.

Michelle: And it's not like, okay, she's good for a woman in leadership, no. She's good in leadership, period! And so, I feel like when women come here, they are empowered by that. You know, she's not afraid to bless her husband ... and makes it quite clear that when they are home, he's priest. And she doesn't try to mix that up. So I think all women who see it, it helps us to feel empowered. To say you know what? Okay. I can step out, I can do that, I can be that and not feel like I have to compromise or feel less than, because I am a woman.

Support

Although women have been fighting for equality throughout the history of humankind, society is ready to take on the gender battle at another level this time around. The landscape is indeed changing for women serving in the capacity of leadership, not just in the marketplace, but also in our churches. Statistical data also supports this notion. Women are completing college at higher numbers and are attending seminary schools by record numbers.[5] And as it relates to church attendance, by in large, women make up the majority of churchgoers on a national scale.[6] The assessments and needs of women have taken center stage with increased research interests of women church leaders in academia, seminary schools, and the medical field.

The vastness and depth of the subject matter warrants a multitude of perspectives to tackle the systemic challenges associated with the topic of gender equality. The emphasis on gender equality has reached a fevered pitch and is demanding a favorable response from influential patriarchs. The church is the perfect environment for this broader gender debate and eventual change. There is great expectation that the church will lead society in implementing equitable treatment toward women, and women leaders in the church are primed to champion this cause. While it would be ideal for church patriarchs to lead the way, we simply can't wait for that. While continued conversation about this topic of women leadership in church is quite helpful, the implementation of drastic change is imminent.

Women, by and large, have the requisite skills to best meet the emotional and social needs of church attendees anyway. If we think of church like parenting (since many times pastors are affectionately referred to as spiritual fathers and mothers), church members would get the best out of their church experiences if men and women were pastoring together. Whether at home or in the church, "children" do best when they have the instruction and guidance from the male *and* female perspective. It doesn't matter if the coleading pastors are married or not. It would just be wise to always have both perspectives involved in the guiding, caring, and decision-making since the outcomes affect both men and women.

Churches have been historically designed and led from a cultural and familial perspective, not a biblical or spiritual one. Western churches have set up a hierarchical organizational system that breeds superiority, with massive opportunities for perversion, pride, fraud, waste, and abuse, just to name a few. If capable, competent women were more visible in our churches and had more prominent authoritative voices in how things were done, we would see an immediate decline in the madness we are witnessing and hearing about in our churches. Of course, this isn't a one-size-fits-all operational suggestion, but it is a thoughtful plea for us to reconsider how we do leadership and reevaluate what we think about the role of women in our churches.

Interestingly, there are two types of organizations that are spearheaded by women who advocate for and against gender equality in the church. Organizations such as Christians for Biblical Equality, the Evangelical and Ecumenical Women's Caucus, and the Women's Ordination Conference work with both Catholic and Protestant churches to elevate equitable practices for both male and female church leaders. Opposing organizations, such as Concerned Women for America and the Council on Biblical Manhood and Womanhood, have fought against equitable practices and instead advocate for the traditional gender roles of males as the leaders and women as the nurturers and supportive help for other women.[7] Both types bolster thousands of members and provide conferences, teachings, and advocacy that support their respective causes.

With so much resistance out there, I would be interested to know how women—who are only responding to their belief that they are called to take on responsibilities in church to strengthen and build up the body of Christ—are faring emotionally, spiritually, and psychologically. Women complain of being demeaned and ridiculed for seeking or accepting leadership roles instead of being supported. I wonder what God thinks about our efforts to snuff out this fire and passion in the women he created as they desire to serve humanity. After all, fundamentally speaking, leadership is about serving and service, right? It's time to come to the table to discuss what's best for the whole, meaning every man and every woman, to see how we can ensure that every woman is being valued, respected, and heard as much as men. I believe God would support such an effort.

Because of the growing failures within our homes, schools, governments, and churches, we need to reexamine where we've missed properly valuing the treasures inside young girls who become grown women. I would venture to say we're missing the creativity, perspective, experience, wisdom, and feminine abilities of Eve within each of us. It's called a woman's touch, and it makes the difference everywhere—it always has. But since it's been devalued and dismissed, it has gravely cost us. The extent of the damage to humankind may never accurately be known.

Thankfully, it's not too late. With urgency, we've got to find our voice and our place, and there is no better time to do it than the present. I've decided I want to support integral and qualified women in leadership, and I'm ready to speak out against inequality in the lives of other women whenever and however the opportunity presents itself. What's your stance?

PART 2

The Explanation

*When you start seeing your worth, you'll find
it harder to stay around people who don't.*
—Unknown

Chapter 5

Identity Crisis Dissected

Women Are Struggling to Find Themselves—Why?

*A*s a social science researcher, I have studied human development from various angles and causations. One such area that I'm fascinated with is *identity*. Who we think we are, what we believe about the world around us, and what we have been able to accomplish (or not) has the power to drive our actions and thoughts every day of our lives. When we are unclear about who we are, it shrouds our ability to confidently navigate our personal journeys through life. Without a sense of identity, we struggle with establishing boundaries and becoming good decision-makers. For this chapter, for us to do a deeper dive into this topic, I've developed working definitions for the following terms *identity, identity conflict*, and *identity crisis*.

The term *identity* can be evaluated from multiple perspectives. It largely depends on the subject matter being discussed. It's my hope that by providing an identity lens for us to utilize, we can carefully consider the impact of these terms relative to this discussion about gender inequality against women leadership in the church. *Identity* is who a person believes himself/herself to be based on associations or group identifications;[1] *identity conflict* is one's lack of clarity pertaining to one's role or purpose in a social or work environment;[2] and *identity crisis* is described as a phase of confusion or uncertainty about one's sense of identity. This occurs when a person becomes insecure as a result of an unexpected change. That change may be directly connected to personal accomplishments or role assignments within certain social relationships (e.g., in families, groups, organizations, occupations, etc.).[3]

The Importance of Identity

Why is identity important? When it comes to human behavior, behaviorists, social science researchers, theorists, and other professionals have long studied the progression of human beings and their development from the time a child is conceived until a person dies, commonly phrased as "cradle to grave." In a process known as *stages of development,*[4] a healthy person will experience and successfully complete nine stages of development, broken down by age groupings. While the groupings are used as signposts to help us study certain behaviors to determine the level of a person's maturation over time, there are still no definitive demarcations that establish if/when a person will successfully navigate from one phase to the other. It is understood, however, that if a person does not successfully progress during these specified timeframes (or stages), an individual will continue to be challenged in that particular developmental area well into adulthood. This delay has the potential of negatively impacting future developmental stages as well as impeding a person's personal and professional relational dynamics. For the sake of time and space, we're only going to review the fifth stage of development, which covers *identity*.

According to Erik Erikson, renowned psychologist and theorist, stage five is prevalent between the ages of twelve and nineteen. This is when an individual is asking herself, "Who am I, and what can I be?" If a person is not able to adequately answer these questions through social relationships with peers and role models, a crisis may arise impacting the person's ability to have clear identity about his or herself, versus experiencing role confusion. Since stage five continues into early adulthood, a person is normally making such decisions like what to study in college, interests, career aspirations, and decisions about the future. Other areas that are impacted include choosing political and religious affiliations, as well as entertaining thoughts about romantic relationships. If stifled in stage five in any way, a person can be severely impeded in his or her emotional, spiritual, occupational, and romantic pursuits.

As women we may struggle with the development of our identity because many of us are either natural nurturers, or we are groomed (through families or social environments) to be concerned about the welfare of others. Whether our motive to help, serve, or give comes from a healthy or unhealthy place, many women still struggle with how to balance giving to others with giving to themselves. We often must be taught how to properly consider ourselves and what we want or need. And unfortunately, many women are not taught to understand who they are as individuals, or what their purpose or calling is on the earth. Our capability to answer these questions about ourselves (or not) will impact our ability to answer every other question we may have about our lives.

In chapter 1, I asked you a series of questions that are geared to help you connect to the passion that's deep inside of you. I asked what do you do when you: (1) have a passion or a sense of duty to *be* something or to *do* something that may be contrary to what others think is right for you (those others could be a boss, coworker, business partner, family member, professor, pastor, friend, or even your spouse); (2) have a burden to go after a skill, a vocation, a career, a business, or anything else that you have been taught is flat-out wrong for you to have—so it causes you to doubt yourself; or (3) believe in your heart that you have been born to pursue a cause beyond your capacity or current abilities? If you were not able to answer them, or your response to any of those questions is a mere, "I don't know," you are suffering from an identity crisis.

Heredity and Environment Work Together

These and many other feelings or beliefs about ourselves are compounded, intensified, accepted, or rebuffed based on our upbringing and biblical understanding of who God has created us to be. If you were raised in a Christian home to believe God's word or have come to believe God's word as an adult, then you know what God says about you supersedes all else. Our ability to accept our greatness and uniqueness is predicated on the dual significance of our genetics and upbringing. One of my professors in undergraduate school at Morgan State University, named Thom Thompson, taught us that, "Heredity and environment are always working together in a complex interrelated way to produce various results." We were required to memorize this statement. I never forgot it because I've seen it play out in people's lives over and over again. How we began in our early developmental years sets the stage for our upward momentum, our destructive downfall, or even worse, our stagnation, resulting in a complete sense of nothingness.

Our social environments are crucial as well. This would include our friends, our coworkers, and our involvement in networks and organizations. This is the point where the church would affect an individual (unless the person spends equal time at church and home), whereby a person no longer realizes where one entity ends and the other begins. If you were raised attending a church that marginalized women, or you attend a church now that marginalizes women, you will struggle with knowing what you should believe about who you are. It's possible the influence of both church and home would be similar since people are most likely influenced by these two entities the most.

Think about it. You either feel great about who you are when you are at home or church, or you feel terribly frustrated or depressed. Do a self-assessment right now. Whether good or bad outcomes, you can thank your families and/or your churches for having an indelible impression on how you see yourself today. For some that may be bad news. The good news is, if you don't like what you discover about yourself, you can always change it! The Bible teaches that change begins with the renewing of your mind (Romans 12:2), and it also explains how we can replace negative thoughts with good thoughts.

Let's look at how each female research participant experienced various aspects of identity in their lives, paying close attention to how their upbringing, church involvement, beliefs, and behaviors influenced how they saw themselves.

First we will look at the participants who felt confident about their identity:

> **Suzanne:** Well, because I grew up in the church, and because the Lord saw fit to give me gifts that could be used for the kingdom, I started very early in the church teaching. And I guess as I look back on it, it was bits of administration back then too. Although I was a teenager, I taught the adult Bible Sunday school when I was thirteen years old in that church.

> **Yvette:** And I think, with my background just growing up as a strong girl who had a voice, and knew I had one, and didn't need people to make me—to even bring me in, which is why I was so content with what I was doing. I didn't need to be in the inner circle.

> **Anna:** I'm at a point in my life; I … don't let things that I cannot change bother me. So all I say is, God, give them revelation. You know … allow me to speak what you want me to say and let me keep moving. So I do that. I don't let that deter me that I will question the call upon my life. And I think that is what the enemy wants us to do when we hear these things, is to begin to question the call upon our lives.

The next two participants show what identity crisis looks like:

> **Michelle:** After graduating high school, I went to college for a couple of years, but I dropped out, after, like, my second year. And it was around that time where I also stopped going to church. And so I was just kind of out there for, like, a few years. I call it my dark years, because I really was just—I didn't know what I was doing.

> **Diane:** And one of the things that I lived with from about the age of thirteen was this fear that I was going to lose them [her parents]. And I did. I did. I lost them very early. I was like twenty-two years old, twenty-four years old. By the time I was twenty-four, they were both gone. So once that happened, I realized I had no one to turn to except the Lord, and so that verse of scripture that says when mother and father forsake me then the Lord will take me up. And so the Lord just opened up doors and put people in my pathway.

And finally, a participant experiencing identity conflict:

> **Judy:** I didn't feel ashamed of my leadership ... because he [her father] told me I had a voice. The frustrating part was when I was in situations where I didn't have a voice, you know. I was the president of my school and middle school and I kept wanting to put myself in places of leadership, but the interesting thing is when I came to the church it was a different— it was a different story and I wrestled with that.

The Identity Struggle Is Real

My research revealed that for many women, the identity challenge is a significant struggle. And although a percentage of women will move forward in their quest to serve as church clergy, many women will instead retreat to more traditional gender roles. The traditional role for women has often been described as that of the helper, which to many means being a support or holding an administrative role in the church. In the home, it means maintaining the home, caring for the children, and assisting the husband in any way necessary. If women are continuously acquiescing to this definition of helper both at home and at church, it confirms existing research data that points to women feeling undervalued and underutilized at church.[5]

In addition, women who defied their traditional role and disclosed to their church leadership that they knew they were called into ministry, felt immediate rejection, which devastated them.[6] The need for validation and acceptance among women in the church is vital. When acceptance is not given, the woman and ultimately the church will have to deal with the adverse effects on women's perceptions of their personal and spiritual identity. Female pastors' conflicts with the church have caused some women's beliefs about God to be tainted. These women may even question their reason for existing and begin to lack confidence in their abilities.

This mistreatment of women has given rise to the growing interpersonal and church conflict among its members, thus also sparking identity conflicts within women about who they are in the eyes of God and their value and contribution to the ministry work of the church. This intensifying conflict has caused women to reevaluate their church involvement. This can serve to be detrimental to the expansion of the church since women make up most of the membership in churches nationwide. Church policies, whether written or normalized through cultural practices, need to be reevaluated to address this long-standing issue about women.

If you've fallen victim to any of these erroneous identity labels, make the choice to reidentify yourself. Environments matter, and we must choose to surround ourselves with people who see in us what God sees. God has made it clear if someone becomes a Christian, he/she is a brand-new person on the inside and is no longer the same (2 Corinthians 5:17). However, for this to be true, you must choose to take on God's new identity for you.

Chapter 6

Power Theory Analysis

Is Power or Service the Driving Force
in Your Quest for Leadership?

*W*hen I hear words such as *rule, control, command,* and *influence* used together, I associate them with one word: *power.*

When I hear words such as *direction, guidance, governance,* and *supervision* used together, I associate them with one word: *leadership.*

When I hear words such as *helping, supporting,* and *assisting* used together, I associate them with one word: *service.*

In an organizational culture where it is chic and applauded to be a servant leader, which means being more people-focused than self-focused or organization-growth focused, it is difficult for me to figure out which emphasis is most important in the Christian church. When I surveyed the twelve participants in my study, the primary description used to define leadership was someone who has influence. Consistently, the word *influence* defined both leadership and power. Based on this information, I was able to make an important connection: the thought of having a female pastor in a position of power or leadership means she is now in a position to influence them. My research findings revealed that most people do not want to be influenced by a woman, period! If you think or feel this way, here is a good time to ask yourself, "Why do I have a problem being influenced by a woman?" When I asked the participants a similar question for the main reasons they opposed, or why they thought others opposed women in leadership, they answered: (a) it wasn't their preference (they preferred a man), (b) it's against the Bible, and (c) women shouldn't lead a man (it's just not right).

From a church perspective, the Bible teaches that the best and greatest way to lead is to serve, not influence. In John 13:12–17, we have the example of Jesus washing the disciples' feet. Once Jesus was done, he wanted them to understand the significance of his actions and to follow the example he had set:

> After he had washed their feet, had put on his robe, and had returned to the table, he said to them, "Do you know what I have done to you? You call me Teacher and Lord—and you are right, for that is what I am. So if I, your Lord and Teacher, have washed your feet, you also ought to wash one another's feet. For I have set you an example, that you also should do as I have done to you. Very truly, I tell you, servants are not greater than their master, nor are messengers greater than the one who sent them. If you know these things, you are blessed if you do them.

How we define leadership is what represents the pendulum between power and service. In fact, one of the greatest characteristics that leadership should ascribe to possess is that of servanthood. Although it sounds lovely, the willingness to serve is hardly the criteria that causes many men *and* women to attack, berate, and sentence any woman to hell who chooses to give her life in service to God by becoming a pastor or any other high-level leader in the church. If we think about it, some of Jesus's most notable leadership characteristics included him being forgiving, compassionate, loving, humble, just, and a servant. In Jesus's quest to promote and demonstrate leadership that represented these qualities, the religious leaders of that day, the Sadducees (upper-class aristocratic priests who did not believe Jesus was the Messiah), the Pharisees (middle-class legalistic traditionalists who did not believe Jesus was the Messiah), and the scribes (authorities on all things related to the scriptures and teachers of the law who did not believe Jesus was the Messiah) all fought persistently to reject, deny, and ultimately kill Jesus for exercising this brand of leadership. These three groups of leaders exuded power and/or influence but were constantly found guilty of having no mercy, justice, or faith (Matthew 23:23). They were especially judgmental and condescending to women (Luke 7, John 8). It's important to note that Jesus constantly admonished these leaders for displaying such negative behaviors against people not like them—especially women.

Power

The most basic definition of power is the ability to influence others. Theorists argue that power is at the center of our human affairs and the hallmark of leadership.[1] In fact, power is believed to be the driving force of leadership. With power playing such a critical role in our human existence, if any group, organization, or society wants to accomplish its goals, or stave off the risk of failure, dysfunction, or destruction, it must solve its problems of power.[2] Let's look here at different types of power:[3]

1. Coercive power—reinforced by fear
2. Connection power—level of influence and interactions with important persons
3. Expert power—degree of knowledge, skills, and competencies
4. Information power—possession of and access to knowledge
5. Legitimate power—based on the leader's position
6. Referent power—personal traits that followers admire or identify with in another
7. Reward power—ability to appoint salaries, advancement, and recognition

Each power type is constantly being played out in the area of our homes, our jobs, our meet-up groups or networks, our communities, or our churches. According to power theory, self-interest actions that leaders capitalize on are based on their followers' self-interests, often using manipulation and persuasion, to aid in the pursuit of their own will and desires. So what exactly does that mean? It means that if you have something that I (as the leader) would like, I'll pretend to care about what you want, so I can ultimately get what I want. For example, some politicians are notorious for this practice. They will make claims and promises that they have no intention to make good on. Nevertheless, they will say whatever is necessary to secure your vote. You give the vote, but the promised action never materializes. For this not to be a person's motivation, a leader must be intentional about not abusing power and recognize the magnitude of responsibility that goes along with having it.

The Bible reminds us that to whom much is given, much is required (Luke 12:48), but most times we're all too busy focusing on the "much is given" part. What we *should* be reminding one another about is the "required" portion which guarantees that one day we will all be giving an account of our actions (Ecclesiastes 12:14, 2 Corinthians 5:10). As leaders our accountability is even higher when we are tasked with teaching others the scriptures (James 3:1) such as in the role of a pastor. Leaders must take great care to not abuse power since we are automatically awarded power when given a leadership title. Power, used responsibly, can become a vital tool for leaders to spearhead any needed changes important in efforts to build, grow, or operate effectively within any organization. If this is true, then the converse is also true. Power used irresponsibly can be an enabling tool in efforts to remain inactive, tear down, suppress, or operate ineffectively within any organization. All these ideas about leadership encompass the authority given through the means of a leader's ability to influence.

Power Theory Analysis

Through my research, I was able to recognize various types of power as listed above which contributed to the ongoing conflict in the churches at the center of this study. The most experienced types of power discussed (whether the participants realized they were discussing each type or not) were *connection* power, *legitimate* power, and *referent* power. Some of the participants spoke of the importance of *connection* power, which was predicated on gaining the approval and favor of the person in power, such as the senior pastor. This is evident today by what women are up against because they are continually looking for their significance from those within the leadership ranks who will validate their right to be in ministry, especially from the senior pastor.

I identified the participants' experiences with *referent power*. This type of power is necessary because people often respond best to those they identify with.[4] Both men and women witnessed a high level of frustration by women congregants when women did not have someone to directly associate or identify with (other female leaders). The women were also frustrated in knowing they possessed a certain gift, skill, or talent that could help others, but they were not able to utilize such gifts simply because of their gender. When *legitimate* power is not bestowed upon those who believe they are qualified to have it, tension and dissatisfaction manifest. I was intrigued with Kevin's thoughts on this issue:

> **Kevin:** I mean, conflict can occur, and it might not necessarily always be conflict, although it could be friction—it could be when there are women that have leadership gifts or teaching gifts and those are being suppressed. That often creates some conflict and angst, and so within the woman herself, who might be really trying to live within the system, and yet that gift just leaks out and people are blessed by that and people are like, let's have some more of that, that's good. Well now I can't have more of that. Why can't we have more of that? So it creates an unnatural condition where somebody's gift is being unnecessarily suppressed.

Theorists surmise that power is bestowed through the empowerment of self and others.[5] Power is a vital tool for leaders to orchestrate much-needed change and to expand old ways of thinking within any organization. Leaders possess a tremendous opportunity to have positive effects on those who are watching to see how leadership is being conducted. As with any significant change, it starts from the top. Cornelius offered a vision of what power and gender equality in leadership can look like when he stated the following:

> **Cornelius:** We're responsible to be here, we're responsible to do that [be there], and he's [the senior pastor] looking at us, you know, because the elder board consists of, there were two men and three women and he still looks to us all as equal and ... he relies on all of us the same.

Leadership

The leadership crisis is inherent in every segment of the professional world.[6] The challenges facing organizations and how to combat them is still a looming question with no clear answers. The need for active and diverse leaders has become a growing topic as the demographics of the United States evolves. Experts explain, "The process of becoming a leader is the process of becoming an integrated human being."[7] The definition of the word *integrated* is to make into a whole by bringing all parts together. When it comes to leadership, what are those parts? In my estimation, the integration includes personal development, which might consist of physical (diet, health, and exercise), spiritual (connection to God), emotional (relationships, mental health), and intellectual (personal and professional development) aspects of a person, as well as interpersonal development encompassing how we engage others. If the marketplace understands that diverse leadership is needed to meet human needs in all these areas, why wouldn't churches also understand that we need to better represent those whom we serve? It just makes sense.

Gender inequality at the highest levels is not just a factor in churches. Faith-based institutions of higher learning (Christian colleges) show the same discrepancies.[8] My research revealed that more women are needed in higher levels of scholastic leadership. Also, women in higher learning are also expressing that they too need to see role models and have access to female mentors in this arena. What's important to note here is that the organizational culture of these colleges was found to be a direct reflection of the affiliated churches to which the academic institution was connected. Here is the takeaway: gender issues are steeped in the religious culture along with hierarchical vying for power and control by the men who are in the highest positions of power.

One of the arguments often made as to why women can't be leaders in churches is due to the failure of Eve. We still make women pay for Eve's sin even though we have all been redeemed by the blood of Jesus Christ. His death, burial, and resurrection has atoned for everything done wrong in the past, giving everyone a fresh start. The Bible declares that what was destroyed by one man, Adam (not the woman), was reestablished by another man, Jesus (Romans 5:12). If this is true, women rightfully resume the power and authority they were created with, right? After all, when men fail as leaders of congregations today because they are, stealing money, committing adultery, taking drugs, watching pornography, or desiring fame from the world at the expense of not caring for the congregation, they are often given passes for their weaknesses, yet women have been forever banished from leading because of Eve's sin. But what about Adam's sin? Somehow, critics would have us believe that God has *only* forgiven Adam for his sin in the garden. Therefore, *only* men are forgiven by God. It sounds so absurd when written down in black and white. Without evidence or cause, many accuse women who desire to lead in the church to be Jezebels, swearing that *any* woman who desires authority over a man is manipulative and power hungry, ready to destroy the church, and going straight to hell. This kind of woman is pegged as being a she-woman, man-hater, who's a defiant, extremist feminist, and above all, *she's out of order*! I have one simple question: Was not the blood strong enough to redeem her as well?

The biggest hypocrisy I found from my research is that no matter what the participants said or even believed, what they did or practiced within their churches didn't quite match their rhetoric. Although they all spoke of equality, none of the churches were completely operating in this belief. But at some point what is said must be challenged, and a subsequent action must follow that exemplifies equality and unity. Otherwise, we are spinning our wheels yet going nowhere. And at the same time, while it may appear that we're not going anywhere, we actually are. We're just not going to the destination that would be most beneficial for women or the Christian church as we know it.

Service

There are other leadership qualities that are also important beyond one's ability to have ultimate authority as exemplified by Jesus. These attributes look more like service. Past researchers have highlighted the different leadership styles between women and men as compared within churches. It is observed that experiences and personalities of women bring a nurturing and comforting aspect to the pastorate.[9] Do you ever question where such characteristics come from? They are God-breathed (Genesis 1:27) and should be accepted, celebrated, and in full operation. And either by biology or socialization, women are perceived as doing ministry better than men. Why? Because by and large, women in church leadership have identified the social and communal aspects of establishing familial-type support to congregants as the leading factors to growth and satisfaction. Supportive characteristics that encourage service come quite naturally to women and are instrumental in fostering hope, love, acceptance, and stability for people who attend church.

The traditional family values highlighting the patriarchal model for both home and church has been the most significant hurdle for women who believe they are called to preach. Many women accept this model but question whether men are operating from a position of competence, strength, and sensitivity to lead in both the home and the church properly.[10] While women may encourage their men to express themselves in ways that are traditionally thought to be womanly (crying in pain and in joy, praying passionately), women themselves have stifled their own power in the process. Women, many of whom "knowingly" submit to the patriarchy, make a sacrifice that involves personal choice. The choice, however, demands a denial of purpose and passion when women forfeit pursuing a calling they believe to be from God.

Does this type of behavior sound familiar? Our churches are filled with men who use their power irresponsibly. The daily news is filled with stories of men who have abused their positions of power, and the collateral damage is horrifying. We see power being used to control and manipulate, not to protect and serve. Pastors have a chance to create opportunities to educate and prepare both men and women who are seeking to serve God through leadership. They just need to be recognized and or developed. Power is also being used to divide instead of unify people. It is the haves and the have nots, and women are systematically left wanting, seeking, and desiring, but rarely obtaining. When the necessity for competent leadership supersedes gender, and one day it will, what will we do with the dogmatic approach to scripture used to suppress women? Here is Kevin again with a viewpoint that gives us a great place to start that dialogue:

> **Kevin:** God's desire was for men and women ... when He gave the sort of cultural mandate [it] ... was given to Adam and Eve together to corule and coreign. And so, then the fall perverted a lot of things, but one of the things that it perverted was the relationship between men and women, and it also perverted people's exercise of power, and those two things have continued to dog the human race throughout time.

Chapter 7

Change Theory Analysis

What Does It Take to Transition When Change Is Inevitable?

*W*hen the Civil Rights Act of 1964 federal law was enacted to fight against discrimination, it originally only covered prejudice in four categories: sex, race, national origin, and religion. Back then it was argued that no one should be denied the right to vote, the right to work, the right to an education, or the right to entrance into public facilities simply based upon the color of their skin or gender. When it came to religion, although it was not a genetic trait, there used to be a time when embracing faith was given great prominence in the United States, so it was important to acknowledge a person's freedom to worship God. The fight for equality seemed impossible to combat. It was brutal, it was lengthy, and it was agonizing—but it was necessary and still continues until this day. Whether people agree or not, this ugly, divisive, and demeaning behavior toward people must change. While this law has not eradicated discriminatory behavior or practices altogether, it's good to know that people have an avenue of recourse to address it.

When considering discrimination, bias, and prejudice in our society, there is an exhaustive array of unprovoked, prohibited, and offensive actions that are happening to people. The reasons for this treatment may or may not be beyond their control: the way they look, talk, behave, walk, laugh, or think. Perhaps it's what people wear, where they live, or who they date; all of these things can be triggers leading to someone being negatively targeted in a hateful manner by another. Such actions are feared and often create hostility, disagreements, or rage about what's not fair, what's illegal, and what's inhumane. Aside from this, scientifically speaking, race (to include your genetic makeup) and gender (to include your genetic makeup) are the two key factors from whence segregation hits people the hardest. Since these behaviors exploit hatred at a high level, we should never see such degrading behavior in our churches. It may not look exactly like this, but segregation of any kind is damaging and does not exemplify the two greatest commandments in the Bible where we are commanded to love God and love others (Matthew 22:36–40).

Change

Let's look at the topic of *change*. Change is defined as the ability to become different or make something different. Depending on the type of change desired, one would have to be intentional about carrying out a new way of thinking, followed by incorporating new routines or habits to get consistent and lasting benefits. Change theory[1] incorporates three stages: (1) The Ending—characterized by confusion about what has ended and what has not; (2) The Neutral Zone—a fuzzy period where the old and new are both in operation; and (3) The New Beginning—the new life is starting, but just as it is unclear what has really ended, it might be equally unclear what has really begun. We will review these stages later in our analysis below.

When going through the stages of change, scholars have detected an internal barrier hindering one's ability to successfully accomplish desired goals. It's called *immunity* to change.[2] This occurs when there is a gap between what is wanted and what can actually be done. We can't figure out why we are struggling to do what we say. The underlying forces to consider for filling such gaps requires addressing the *hidden competing commitments*. These are the many ideas associated with an established way of doing things that makes a person believe it is vital to act in a certain way. Then, there are the *underlying assumptions* made about why certain thoughts or behaviors are necessary.

In chapter 6, I listed three main reasons why some church leaders oppose women in leadership. They are, (a) it isn't their preference (they prefer a man), (b) it's against the Bible, and (c) women shouldn't lead a man (it's just not right). These ideas are all connectors to underlying assumptions when it's assumed that God did not call women to preach, or men make better pastors than women. If a church is working to change this way of thinking about women, even when they are speaking as if they are fully supportive of women in ministry, they will have to address both their hidden competing commitments and their underlying assumptions.

Change Theory Analysis

Scholars[3] believe change theory can be analyzed through a person's process of transition which happens during various phases in life: as an individual, within a relationship, or in a family, a community, or an organization. The stages of change which are the ending, the neutral zone, and the new beginning can be applied in varying degrees at various levels. As I applied change theory to the experiences of my research participants, the findings were quite interesting. Let's look at what occurred with Yvette in her personal life story.

Stage One: The Ending

Yvette told of an experience she had with her brother, who is a pastor. When Yvette was first asked to become an elder at her church, she shared the news with her family. Her brothers and her father, who were all pastors in the Baptist church, told her, "Absolutely not!" She was not to take the elder position, and if she did, they would not support her. And they didn't. When she decided to take the position, the male family members cut her off. Yvette had grown up in an environment where the men were supposed to be in charge at home and in the church. They rejected her deviation from their norm. From that day on, she was not able to tell them the exciting things God was doing through her life as an elder. What used to be weekly family gatherings turned into sporadic holiday get-togethers. Because of the strain on the relationship, Yvette could never discuss what she was doing or get their advice as she navigated this new and challenging terrain. Not too many years later, those men would return to her for advice. The inevitability of change necessitated a different response from her male family members when they found themselves in a similar situation concerning women in their churches. Yvette confided:

> My brother, the biggest hindrance for me, had called me on the phone and said, "You know I have something I want to talk to you about." And we had been talking, but again we never mentioned this [her elder role in the church] ... I knew ... some good things that had happened for me ... I couldn't share with him because he wasn't in a place to receive it. But that was okay. I knew that [it was] his journey that he had to take ... So he says, "You know the Lord is really telling me"—and he's a pastor—he says, "that we need to add women to our council." That's what he called it. I could have just fell out, and I knew it was a God moment! Only God could do that because he [her brother] was just, "Oh no, we don't do this, you know, you're going to hell." And so, I was able to receive that, I cheered him on, and since then we've talked about why he made that decision. I talked to him about it that day, and I said, "Well you know"—and I tried to give him some ... inside help on how to present it ... He was on the front lines of throwing stones at me, [but] I just told him ... "You know you're going to need to walk it out, you're going to need to preach about it ... And you're going to need to have

your position paper, be able to sit down and talk to
people and shepherd people through this because
this is going to be a change." I mean he came right
[out] of [name of university], you know, doctorate
and all that kind of stuff and I said, "This is going
to be a change." So I mean now he's got women in
the pulpit preaching and I'm like, "Oh look at you!"
But I never condemned him for that. I knew it was
a journey that he would need to take on his own.
I didn't know where he would end up, but I know
God did this.

It was a good thing that Yvette had some experience with
knowing what was needed to prepare a congregation for a change
as significant as incorporating women into leadership positions.
She was able to provide her brother with sound guidance to
diminish the amount of confusion he could have experienced. She
was able to help her brother's plan go as smoothly as possible. Let's
not forget that it was also a good thing she was not a mean-spirited
woman. Although her pastor-brother treated her badly, she did not
repay him evil for evil. Through her demonstration of love, she has
provided us with such a beautiful lesson in forgiveness. Whether
you're male or female, you can learn mercy from Yvette's story.

As individuals or organizations go through the three stages
of change, leaders need to be determined to establish a process
that eliminates confusion and resistance as much as possible from
the beginning. It is true, change can be scary and devastating.
Admittedly, there are numerous unknown variables at play,
many of which you can't control or stop. From my research, two
of the three churches reported a significant negative impact from
their decisions to incorporate women as church leaders. When
change is not handled properly, which is a primary culprit for
why many people are hesitant to embrace it, the casualties can be
overwhelming.

James, an executive pastor at a large church, candidly
described a dreadful scenario resulting from his church's poor
implementation of adding women leaders to the elders' board. The
decision to add women as elders was determined after the all-male

leadership team had taken two years to do a thorough doctrinal study on women, eventually concluding that women should be allowed to lead. Even though they hired a consultant to guide them through the doctrinal research aspect of their transition, the leadership team at James's church failed to implement an effective strategy to roll out communication of this decision:

> [Consultant's name] was with us during the whole conversation about doctrine and us walking through the scriptures together, but the lead pastor wasn't really a good process person, and so we didn't take the same amount of time, the same level of intentionality with the process rollout [to tell the congregation about the new female elders being ordained] as we did with how much time we spent with the topic [women leaders in the Bible], and that was the error. I've heard a lot of people were wounded [upon hearing women would be ordained as elders], and we confessed and repented and asked for forgiveness ... and so the conflict ... it was really a two-punch issue ... we could have, maybe rolled it out in a different way.

The church leadership had to go into damage control to try to stop the ongoing pain and confusion the church members were experiencing resulting from how they had learned that women would be serving as elders. Hundreds of people angrily left the church over the fiasco created surrounding the botched rollout. The leadership team was not afforded the benefit of having a knowledgeable person to provide guidance in how best to prepare the congregation for these historic leadership changes, and it cost them greatly. Although the leaders were glad to have made the significant change and have since seen extraordinary results from it, James admitted that they did not handle the transition properly. He described how the leadership team tried to correct their poor communication errors with the congregation:

Well, we went back and realized our error [in not telling the congregation in advance of the leadership change] and really very humbly, we were broken and humbled, and confessed, asked for forgiveness from the whole congregation and from the different people. We ended up having meetings to talk through [the change], which should have come before [the leadership change announcement], so it was post [after the leadership change announcement] ... just to explain how we got, where we got, what the process was ... how we got where we were theologically and those [meetings] were very challenging because you had people in there that [retorted], "what are you doing to our church," and "you're destroying it," and you know, it was just a real issue. It was a very hard time.

Stage Two: The Neutral Zone

My findings revealed that change has been slow to nonexistent in the actions, thoughts, and elevation of women leaders within our churches nationwide. The majority of the research participants agreed that change in the Christian church is way behind progress, even though tremendous progress is being made for women in the marketplace. While some were optimistic about the future of the church, others seemed ambivalent. The unstableness of stage two, the neutral zone, was best illustrated from the experience offered by Suzanne, whose husband serves as pastor, as she explained how her church had dealt with congregants after they chose to add the elder position in their leadership hierarchy which included her and other women as elders. They were dealing with two new changes at once. Suzanne stated:

So our church has been through—or is going through a metamorphosis. We've had some fallout, meaning we've had people leave our church. Although, during the two years that we were training to be elders, we also put the church through training sessions. We had people come in from the outside to teach the biblical principles of eldership in the church. And they taught from Titus [a book in the Bible]. They taught from Timothy [a book in the Bible]. All the— you know, all biblically based. And you can do that. Number one, most of the church did not come out for the training sessions. They didn't feel the need to do that. Number two, they could come out and still not accept the training or accept the word of God as written in the holy scriptures. Number three, they thought it was going to change the way they did church. And some of them have left because they're not willing to change. Or they're not willing to see what changes would occur, if any. Some people, when you talk about change, they run. I say you cannot grow without changing.

Suzanne's church attempted to provide the necessary biblical training on the use of elders and the institution of women as elders prior to the ordination ceremony. Senior leadership thought this was the best way to handle the change so that their members would understand what was going to happen, but the training wasn't well received. As Suzanne's husband/pastor instituted elders, which he believed would prove beneficial for their members, the leadership staff wanted to assure the members that not much would be changing in how church services were conducted.

However, the people who disagreed with the need for the change were not willing to stick around to see if the change would prove disastrous, as they suspected. Like Suzanne, leaders must be convinced that the decision to do something new and different is necessary, and then be willing to stay the course. The accurate assessment of one's readiness to change is paramount for the change to be accepted and to last.[4]

Stage Three: The New Beginning

Judy, along with three other research participants, was a member of a church who was experiencing stage three of change theory. This was the same church that had barely come through the tumultuous transition of adding women to the elders' board many years prior, as described above by James. With the new women elders now solidly in place, the church leaders were beginning to focus on other cemented views about women that also needed to change. Judy shared there were talks about the need to shift mindsets around the acceptance of a woman as senior pastor, not just as elders.

Another necessary change being contemplated was the need to intentionally pursue more women for the elders' board. They had only added two women: one white and one African American woman to a board of a dozen all-white men. She also confided that they needed to ordain and maintain more minority leaders in general. She argued church leadership needed to figure out an effective process that would result in ongoing progress in these areas. She was concerned that there would be no consistent momentum. And without calculated efforts, Judy feared their church would eventually fall back into old norms. She wanted there to be a real heart change about ordaining women, and she didn't want this major accomplishment to become minimized and seen only as a gender quota to please the people.

Kevin, a former pastor at the same church, gave his thoughts on the need to incorporate women in a more purposeful way. He summed up his thoughts with a prediction about the Christian church in general if change about women in leadership remains mishandled:

> Conflicts in the church don't happen because women are serving in leadership. Conflicts in the church happen because we're sinners and because we resist change ... generally people are resistant to change and so, you know, I'd say that women exercising their leadership might become a flashpoint for an issue but it's not the real issue. The real issue is something deeper ... So if we want to be Romans for the sake that all people might know Christ, then to act in the way that is so counter to the culture that the culture is much more affirming and embracing and releasing than the church might be, cripples the church's

witness and further marginalizes a church's ability
to be a transformative presence in its community.

Other Barriers to Change

It's important to share the hard parts about implementing high-
level change because we live in a society that doesn't like pain. We
do everything to numb ourselves, escape, or deny that something
is wrong, uncomfortable, or ineffective. There is a propensity
to focus only on positive responses to change, which can turn
out to be missed opportunities to understand the presence of
negative reactions, such as competition, anger, and resistance.[5]
This was also evident during my interviews when many of the
participants initially only shared the good aspects of change that
were occurring regarding women in leadership positions. However,
the more we talked, the more they revealed their deeper problems
and concerns.

I discovered the central reason why men and women become
paralyzed when questioned or challenged about the need for
the church to evolve and fully embrace women. It's because of
the symbolic sanctity of patriarchal governance that has been
cherished for centuries. Let's face it—the church relishes male
dominance dogma whether it's working or not. As much as many
of us need to believe that God has anointed the male as the only
suitable being to lead or teach the scriptures to church attendees,
is it at all possible that we have become entrenched in an ideology
that limits God's ability to perform amazing and phenomenal feats
through anyone he chooses? God forbid!

Here is a good place to consider the teachings of Jesus as
it relates to how self-aggrandizing, self-appointed men made
decisions about what was right, wrong, clean, defiled, permissible,
or forbidden (Mark 7:1–23 NKJV):

> Then the Pharisees and some of the scribes came
> together to Him, having come from Jerusalem.
> Now when they saw some of His disciples eat bread
> with defiled, that is, with unwashed hands, they

found fault. For the Pharisees and all the Jews do not eat unless they wash their hands in a special way, holding the tradition of the elders. When they come from the marketplace, they do not eat unless they wash. And there are many other things which they have received and hold, like the washing of cups, pitchers, copper vessels, and couches. Then the Pharisees and scribes asked Him, "Why do Your disciples not walk according to the tradition of the elders, but eat bread with unwashed hands?" He answered and said to them, "Well did Isaiah prophesy of you hypocrites, as it is written: 'This people honors Me with their lips, but their heart is far from Me. And in vain they worship Me, teaching as doctrines the commandments of men.' For laying aside the commandment of God, you hold the tradition of men—the washing of pitchers and cups, and many other such things you do." He said to them, "All too well you reject the commandment of God, that you may keep your tradition. For Moses said, 'Honor your father and your mother'; and, 'He who curses father or mother, let him be put to death.' But you say, 'If a man says to his father or mother, "Whatever profit you might have received from me is Corban"—' (that is, a gift to God), then you no longer let him do anything for his father or his mother, making the word of God of no effect through your tradition which you have handed down. And many such things you do." When He had called all the multitude to Himself, He said to them, "Hear Me, everyone, and understand: There is nothing that enters a man from outside which can defile him; but the things which come out of him, those are the things that defile a man. If anyone has ears to hear, let him hear!" When He had entered a house away from the crowd, His disciples asked Him concerning the parable. So He said to them, "Are you thus without understanding also? Do you not perceive that whatever enters a man from outside cannot defile him, because it does not enter his heart but his stomach, and is eliminated, thus purifying all foods?" And He said, "What comes out of a man, that defiles a man. For from within, out of the heart of men, proceed evil thoughts, adulteries, fornications, murders, thefts, covetousness, wickedness, deceit, lewdness, an evil eye, blasphemy, pride, foolishness. All these evil things come from within and defile a man."

Jesus was known for breaking religious traditions. He was concerned about the wickedness in the hearts of humankind, especially the religious leaders of that day. As was the case in the Bible, Jesus is still focused on the intent behind our actions and the depth of our commitment to obey *God's* commands. But just as was true in this passage, our churches are filled with people who want to pay homage to "a way," "a look," and "a feeling." It doesn't matter if our actions hurt or isolate a segment of people. Church leaders are more committed to what *they* believe is right instead of what *God* says is right.

Our own church traditions, which have been handed down from generation to generation, often take priority over God's word. Many churches believe that what they teach about women is doctrine. But in actuality, it's the commandments of men that dictate their actions. You would think that this is an archaic and bombastic way of thinking, but it's still happening today.

The church idolizes the symbolism of the male pastor in the front of the church. He's often referred to as the "man of God." In the eyes of many, he possesses great strength and power like no other. He's seen as a spiritual father figure, a protector and provider, all-wise, all-knowing, and to be handled with kid gloves. Members come to love, honor, and cherish their pastors in a way that can be quite unsettling. Nevertheless, this symbol is a mighty one, an idol of sorts. Now, is there any real power in this male symbol? Yes, the power we choose to give it.

When considering the church as an organization, it has become common vernacular to refer to one's church as one's tribe.

Theorists suggest when an organization sees itself in this manner, it is less likely to subscribe to rules and polices as is the process for providing managerial authority. Instead, churches or tribes adhere more to rituals and ceremonies, leaving too much room for lack of accountability and unfair practices. This has become quite dangerous and church members are growing increasingly discontented. Scholars Bolman and Deal describe it this way: "Organization is also theater: actors play their roles in an ongoing drama while audiences form impressions from what they see on stage. Problems arise when actors blow their parts, symbols lose their meaning, or ceremonies and rituals lose their potency."[6] Does this sound all too familiar? The truth of the matter is church as theater is not working anymore. In many of our churches the "actors" are tired. The symbols are being exposed as hypocrites, and the ceremonies and rituals are proving to be performance-based and not Spirit-led.

Can we admit that something is severely wrong in our churches? I firmly believe many church leaders and members just aren't quite sure what to do. Ignoring the problem is not the answer, and unfortunately, prayer alone will not fix it. Acknowledgment of the need for a change is an excellent first step because what we won't first admit, we cannot heal. I caution us against the desire to pretend all is well by finding a scripture to quote, thereby abdicating ourselves or our leaders of any responsibility to change. It's just a matter of time before the pain of the people spills out into the streets. Without real change, our personal well-being, the health of our families, and the unity of our congregations will continue to be negatively impacted.

My decision to focus on change theory to draw attention to what is happening in our churches is not just to have an intellectual diatribe. It is to sound the alarm that the Christian church seems unwilling to embrace change in the areas of fully recognizing, embracing, and positioning women in leadership. Hidden competing commitments that are currently impeding this inevitable change may prove to be difficult to tackle, but they are not impossible to overcome. No doubt about it, change is hard. But if it is embraced, and you're willing to do the work, change can be good.

Chapter 8

Mental Model Theory Analysis

Are Perspective and Preference
Learned Behaviors?

Mental Model

A mental model is a navigation map in your head, and it determines how you will behave.[1] Researchers say this navigation map is a set of ideas and assumptions you carry in your head to help you understand and negotiate a particular territory. A territory can be a spiritual territory, a financial territory, a marriage territory, a job territory, a friendship territory, a commitment territory, etc. These responses are automatic, without any premeditated thought or consideration. The concept of a frame of mind is a mental model. Have you ever heard someone say, "I'm not in the right frame of mind to ... (do a specific thing)," or "What frame of mind was she in ... (before she left the house, before she left the marriage, before she left the church)?" There are good frames and there are bad frames, most of which are learned behaviors. Your frames are your perspectives—how you see or interpret things.

Perspective

Perspective is mostly learned through receiving teachings or having experiences that assist you in formulating a belief about something. All perspectives can change based on new teachings or new experiences. Sickness, death, tragedy, loneliness, marriage, having children, moving to a new state or country, disappointment, a chance encounter with someone, technology, a new or ending relationship, or significant opportunities in your life can all promote changed or new perspectives.

I found it fascinating that the research participants who attended the same church often shared similar preferences and perspectives about women. I also found it interesting that there were commonalities among all the women's description of women leaders, yet there was a divergence of ideas about women leaders expressed by the men. In most cases, I found that the men were not as descriptive about the positive attributes of women leaders as the women were. I also found that the women were more apt to make excuses for men's gender biases as they discussed the unfair treatment of women obtaining acceptance as leaders. But the men, no matter which side they fell on, were unapologetically willing to defend their stance on the rightness or wrongness of women in leadership. Grouped by their church affiliations, below I list some of the comments made by the participants when they were asked the question, "What are the differences between having a female leader and a male leader in the church?"

Church A

> **Suzanne:** I know that women can be as effective and sometimes more effective [than men]. We're very influential people. Women, they have a God-given gift of influence, sometimes more than a man. I just never had that kind of belief that a man is for leadership and the woman is for something less.

Bill: I don't see any difference. Because I know one woman who is pretty strong—actually, I know a few who are pretty strong—and no, I don't see any difference.

Cornelius: I think sometimes it's just a matter of emotions and internalizing. I think that sometimes when it comes to some issues, men tend to be able to say what needs to be said and move on, but because of the fact that I feel that women are more emotional, they hang on [to] something and don't move on.

Diane: I believe women are very creative. They're very active. They can do anything that the Lord empowers them to do. And I think that the—not to sound prejudiced, but I think a lot of times the creativity is centered in the women in the church. We're the ones who, because of our experiences as nurturers, we're the ones that often times see the broader picture and what has to be done and are willing to go out there and do that.

Church B

James: I feel like it's so important to have both [men and women] complementing one another, and so even if you have a male leader, having female leadership nearby or vice versa, partnering, is really helpful, because you're getting then the fullness, as we talked earlier, of attributes and the characteristics of God, because he is both male and female.

Yvette: Now are you talking temperament wise or—because I think that those are—I think temperament, it would be different. Visually it would be different. And I think that would be the hardest thing that people would not be able to visually accept. It just wouldn't work because we're not there yet ... Men are seen as strong. Men are seen as, get to it, do it, get it done. Women are kind of seen as temperamental.

Kevin: I think each leader is going to bring their own unique set of gifts and abilities and weaknesses to that, and I think that it would be inaccurate to attribute a certain set of strengths, abilities, weaknesses, or even leadership style to a man or to a woman ... I think it's those kinds of stereotypes that perpetuate unevenness and injustice.

Judy: I don't know if it's male or personality, but I think it can be both probably, but I would say the men in our leadership are a little bit—and it's getting better—the processes are getting better. But it's been kind of ready, fire, aim, and deal with the consequences later. I think when a woman is leading, there is much more thought on the process that will get you to a really good conclusion.

Church C

Anna: Females pay closer attention to detail. And we're more sensitive to the needs of a congregation than men. So I think that's the difference; [it] is sensitivity. I think also females have a tendency to be open with their love for people and not so much guarded like men are.

Marcus: None. A good leader is a good leader ... They got the same gifts.

Michelle: I think men are more matter-of-fact. They have less patience with foolishness. They don't like excuses, and they want you to be a person of your word. So, if you say you're going to do x, y, z ... you execute. I think women, we tend to be a little more nurturing. Like, we will give you the truth, but we will follow it up with encouragement.

Antonio: I don't really see any limitations as far as a female pastor.

These responses, while encouraging and supportive of women, did not match subsequent arguments made by the participants about what is required to be a "qualified" leader in the church. In response to questions that centered on "who does it better" (men or women), some of the men participants used gender to rule women out. They argued that they embrace leadership from the spiritual approach as referenced in scripture found in 1 Timothy and 1 Corinthians, which they believe designate men as the head.

With additional probing, I also asked the participants how they defined *church ministry*. Their culmination of responses, of which many were the same, said church ministry is primarily helping people with emotional, relational, physical, mental, financial, educational, and medical needs. Based on their definitions of church ministry, I think it's worth noting that it doesn't appear that gender would be a necessary qualifier to serve as a leader in providing people with these services. Here is my question: if church ministry encompasses both spiritual and natural components, shouldn't there be competent spiritual leaders, both male and female, equipped to meet this mammoth list of needs? My findings demonstrated that there has been minimal progress made toward changing inferior perspectives or adopted preferences about women leaders and the value they add to any organization, especially the church. Let me say more about preferences.

Preference

Unlike perspectives, preferences may not necessarily be taught, but they can certainly be biased, meaning someone chooses one thing or person over another based on unfair reasons or judgments that are not necessarily true or have been personally experienced by that person. A preference is having a greater like of one thing over another. An *unbiased* preference can be in the way you wear your hair, types of food you like, your clothing style, travel destinations you pick, or the types of movies, books, or music you select. These selections can be made objectively and impartially, based on what you personally like. But a *biased* preference, which would denote having partiality toward one thing over another based on a preconceived notion you believe to be true, would be the reasons you give for why a particular ethnic group is late or early to an event; the opinions you have about a person or group based on their political affiliation; or beliefs you hold about short or tall people. It could be the reasons you give for choosing the type of man or woman you will date or marry—for example, selecting a mate based only on ethnic characteristics (hair type, facial features, eye color). Or an example that is important to this discussion, perhaps the rationale you give for who you believe can lead you most effectively is based solely on gender.

To check your unconscious biases, you need self-awareness and thoughtful critiques about why you do what you do, or believe what you believe, to keep overt bias and unconscious bias in check. Decisions that will impact the church, and ultimately the kingdom of God, should not be based on our own thoughts, feelings, wants, desires contrived by decisions such as gender, nationality, denominational differences, etc. We should be operating the affairs of the church with the mind of Christ leading us. Let's consider the following scriptures as we determine to become more self-aware:

> However, brothers and sisters, I could not talk to
> you as to spiritual people, but [only] as to worldly
> people [dominated by human nature], *mere* infants
> [in the new life] in Christ! I fed you with milk,
> not solid food; for you were not yet able *to receive*

it. Even now you are still not ready. You are still worldly [controlled by ordinary impulses, the sinful capacity]. For as long as there is jealousy and strife *and* discord among you, are you not unspiritual, and are you not walking like ordinary men [unchanged by faith]? For when one *of you* says, "I am [a disciple] of Paul," and another, "I am [a disciple] of Apollos," are you not [proving yourselves unchanged, just] *ordinary* people? What then is Apollos? And what is Paul? Just servants through whom you believed [in Christ], even as the Lord appointed to each his task. I planted, Apollos watered, but God [all the while] was causing the growth. So neither is the one who plants nor the one who waters anything, but [only] God who causes the growth. He who plants and he who waters are one [in importance and esteem, working toward the same purpose]; but each will receive his own reward according to his own labor. For we are God's fellow workers [His servants working together]; you are God's cultivated field [His garden, His vineyard], God's building. (1 Corinthians 3:1–9 AMP)

Think about it—if our mental model is as Paul describes here, where people are making decisions about who to follow based on gender or someone's personality, we're being biased. We're being prejudiced. As it relates to the modern-day church, it would mean we believe that God prefers one gender in leadership over the other. The goal of both genders, as ministers of reconciliation and ambassadors of Christ (2 Corinthian 5:14–21), is to be a spokesperson for the primary purpose of either introducing someone to Jesus or teaching someone about the principles of Jesus. If Jesus is our example, he used the least likely women to carry his message. And he chose the least likely women to work alongside him in ministry. Based upon what Paul is saying here, biased behavior is quite immature and even unspiritual! God's desire is that none should perish (2 Peter 3:9), and he'll use anyone or anything to accomplish that.

Consider Philippians 3:12–20 (AMP):

> Not that I have already obtained it [this goal of being Christlike] or have already been made perfect, but I actively press on so that I may take hold of that [perfection] for which Christ Jesus took hold of me *and* made me His own. Brothers and sisters, I do not consider that I have made it my own yet; but one thing *I do*: forgetting what *lies* behind and reaching forward to what *lies* ahead, I press on toward the goal to win the [heavenly] prize of the upward call of God in Christ Jesus. All of us who are mature [pursuing spiritual perfection] should have this attitude. And if in any respect you have a different attitude, that too God will make clear to you. Only let us stay true to what we have already attained. Brothers and sisters together follow my example and observe those who live by the pattern we gave you. For there are many, of whom I have often told you, and now tell you even with tears, who live as enemies of the cross of Christ [rejecting and opposing His way of salvation], whose fate is destruction, whose god is *their* belly [their worldly appetite, their sensuality, their vanity], and *whose* glory is in their shame—who focus their mind on earthly *and* temporal things. But [we are different, because] our citizenship is in heaven.

As Christians we are admonished to be disciplined and mature in our thoughts, keeping our focus on what's important to God, not man. Here is the kicker: if you have a different thought about women that is contrary to God's thoughts about women, it is incumbent upon you to renew your mind and refrain from succumbing to your personal biases.

Mental Model Theory Analysis

As stated before, in its purest form, a church is an organization. Within the church organization there are ministries (teams or groups) with their individual and corporate mentalities that comprise perspectives, understandings, and imaginations that may or may not be true. The church's organizational culture and the connected mentalities are exemplified and reinforced by those who are given various levels of authority. Scholars[2] believe there is a direct correlation between personality, degree of social interaction, and the way one thinks (mental model). These variables together dictate how decisions are made and how conflict is addressed. Why is this significant? Because, whatever you believe, you need to be able to rightly defend those beliefs based on the word of God.

As Christians, we need to fully understand what the scriptures mean, not just what we've been told. The Bible says we are to be like the Bereans and study the Bible for ourselves (Acts 17:11). Cults, clubs, and secret societies are all built on common core beliefs. Those who join them are willing to accept and echo the words that are espoused by the leaders of these groups, without challenging ideas that seem questionable. Remember, as human beings, one of our greatest assets is our minds. It gives us our ability to choose, to think freely, and to challenge and question *anything* that doesn't makes sense when we're experiencing it through our five senses (see, hear, smell, taste, touch). We should never give up our God-given rights to think and have an opinion. God desires to reason with us. He supports us having questions, curiosity, and challenges to what's said (Isaiah 1:18; Matthew 15:21–28).

Whenever you find yourself in a situation where you are reprimanded or chided for expressing concern, requiring more information before agreeing to something, or feeling uneasy about events, activities, ideologies, or demands on you, use your free will to remove yourself from such bondage. Yes, it's bondage! As a rule of thumb, when your freedom is in jeopardy or you are made to feel like your questions or doubts about something being done is proving your inability to trust or have faith in someone, that's a red flag. Be alert to signs of control, manipulation, or justifications to excuse any of the following: wrongdoing, oppressive behavior, or shortcuts to established Bible processes. You must have standards. That means don't participate in lying, cheating, stealing, or any other behaviors found in Galatians 5:19–21.

This takes us back to Genesis. Since the beginning of time, man and woman have had an enemy. In the New Testament, Jesus teaches that our enemy's primary agenda is to steal, kill, and destroy (John 10:10). Our enemy has worked overtime to use contentious tactics to keep men and women divided. To reverse the negative effects this has caused, we have to change our mind about our approach toward one another.

Our perspectives should be based on what God says about us. But here is the tricky part: God speaks through people, and we have to be vigilant in testing what we hear before we accept what we are being told. In the same way you have minds and your five senses to get the full experiences out of life, you need to use your minds and your five senses to properly understand what God had in *his* mind when he created you. No one person, scripture, or experience can dictate all of who you are or what you can do. No longer allow *anyone* to feed you a few scriptures that have been erroneously applied to oppress women. We must use all resources together to create a complete picture for ourselves.

Remember, heredity and environment are always working together in a complex, interrelated way to produce various results. So here's my point: if you attend a church that discriminates against women, your opportunities will be limited and your image of yourself will be limited. If you attend a church where they believe women are equal in ability and calling, your opportunities will be limit*less*, and your image of yourself will be enlarged. It's the same with marriages, jobs, and any other scenarios that impact or influence a person's thoughts about him/herself. As hard as it is to leave beloved churches, family churches, controlling churches, or popular churches, if you are not getting what you need to develop as an individual, to become what God intended, find strength in knowing that your right to choose for yourself is your greatest weapon. Use it. According to the Bible, you alone will stand before God to give an account for how you chose to multiply the talents he gave you (Matthew 25:13–40).

We live in a world of self-generating beliefs that remain largely untested. And people are the embodiment of what they think. Until we want to change, we're not going to change. All thoughts will remain etched in our hearts until we renew our minds. To bring this chapter to a close, I want to take you back into the psyche of the research participants.

As the conversation about women leadership continued during my interviews, thoughts became a little more reflective about injustices women have fallen victim to in the church. My understanding of mental modeling helped me to recognize thought patterns participants had developed over time. Most of the participants had their own secret perspectives that were still influencing their thoughts about the Christian church's stance on women, where we are as an organization, what got us here, and what will move us forward.

Church A

>   **Suzanne:** Anytime you create change from tradition, you're going to have some people who try to embrace it. But a lot of times, you have more that try to hold on to tradition.

>   **Bill:** In my church, not a problem. They accept whatever direction I set forth. And I don't say that arrogantly—I'm thirty-one years old now [years of pastoring], so they're basically going to embrace what I embrace. And those who don't, they'll go where they're comfortable.

>   **Cornelius:** Just based on my interpretation of the scriptures, I will hold to the doctrine of 1 Timothy. He who desires the office of the bishop ... must be the husband of one wife, and I just hold on to that.

Diane: Well if I feel small, I want you to feel small too. My husband always likens it to crabs in a barrel. We constantly want to pull each other down. I don't want you to get to the top because I'm at the bottom, so I'm going to make sure that you don't get any further.

Church B

James: I think that again, we get stuck in our religiosity, we get stuck in our theological viewpoints and ways of doing what we're doing, and we just keep doing it. We just keep repeating.

Yvette: Yeah, I think it's an unconscious thing that, you know, even—let's just take the group of elders for instance. Even though they wanted you there and they could value you being there, it was still like I said, that good old boy kind of thing. Or when you're speaking something, they just kind of talk right over you and never realize that that's what they do because it is just engrained in them.

Kevin: And so I think that people, you know, cannot even say why they think a woman should or shouldn't be in a particular role, I mean because most people haven't thought about it deeply. They experience it or as it came upon them, they had a visceral reaction to it [women becoming elders], and then the logical side of their brain tried to explain the visceral reaction that they were having ... It's sort of a neurological, emotional explanation of human behavior.

Judy: But I don't think—I just don't think it's intentional thought, I don't think it's—there are some churches that are thinking that way but it's oftentimes the super-liberal churches, right, Episcopalians, you know, Anglicans don't even, but, I know Episcopalians and Methodists and some Lutherans, you know, Presbyterians and people, you know, so I think it's just a lack of thought about it. I just don't think—I don't think that men think about it, women think about it, but I don't think that men do and until the men do, probably, and say hey, hey, hang on, this is not right [how women are treated].

Church C

Anna: The mindset of a lot of men is they cannot sit under a woman pastor because of some writings that Paul did in the book of Corinthians and I think the book of Timothy where he addressed women in leadership.

Marcus: And I feel that—and not just men, there are some ladies out there that feel that they shouldn't have a woman leader.

Michelle: I really think if people could get—if we—if people could get away from their prejudices, we would all be the better for it. You know? I really think, like, and I guess it takes looking at things from a different perspective, because I really feel like you shoot yourself in the foot when you don't allow people to, not just only be who they are but to help them excel and be the best that they can be.

Antonio: Most people who come into the congregation are not even interested in the business part of the church ... They may come to worship, but when it comes to the business portion ... looking at the church policy and legislation and laws, it's,

"Oh no, I'm not called to do that." But they may
say, "Okay, I don't like that. I don't see any women
bishops." But [my question is], are you willing to
challenge that and send that information forward
and challenge the leadership to change the laws
and bylaws …? Are you willing to say, "You better
do something to get more women into this?" You
know, it's like, is the church really up to challenge
those type laws to bring about the change.

The research findings shared in part 2 of this book are
instrumental in gaining a broader perspective of how power,
change, and mental model theories highlight the underlying
ideologies and philosophies that have the potential of hindering our
individual and corporate progress as the Christian church. To be
effective at an optimum level, churches and church leaders would
be remiss to not engage in this complex conversation regarding
women leadership.

The growing stance of women is that churches need to
have both genders functioning in leadership roles. The choice
to embrace or refute this reality may directly correlate to the
extent that women consider their church involvement as relevant
to their spiritual growth; the church's level of effectiveness to meet
the needs of its members; or the perceived long-term importance
of churches overall in decades to come. To make such a drastic
shift, the church must choose to reconcile the needs and callings
of women against traditional thinking that has resulted in the
version of the church in operation today.

PART 3

The Resolution

*When there is no enemy within, the
enemies outside cannot hurt you.*

—AFRICAN PROVERB

Chapter 9

Confronting the Elephant in the Church

We Cannot Change What We Will Not First Acknowledge

*N*ow that we've discussed various elements of "The Conflict" in part 1 and considered dimensional complexities of "The Explanation" in part 2, part 3 is an opportunity for us to evaluate our own practices in relation to our level of comfort (or lack thereof) in confronting the gender debate regarding women in church leadership. This is the proverbial elephant in the room. We need to do an honest assessment of our personal beliefs about this topic. In my opinion, it is by far the biggest elephant our churches must face.

What we choose to do with the information provided in these pages will either help or hinder our ability to close the growing chasm that is developing between men and women in our churches. How Christian women choose to respond to the gender leadership debate will negatively or positively impact many of those who look to the church for relational, moral, and spiritual guidance. Our reaction can no longer be to ignore this problem. That has not worked. We must open our hearts, have the conversation, review the scriptures more closely (with scriptural and intellectual honesty), and then be brave enough to prayerfully make whatever changes we believe we need to make for the greater good of women and our churches.

God Doesn't Need Men's Permission

As Christian churches continue to quietly wrestle with where they stand on the topic of women in ministry, women can be grateful that God doesn't need men's permission to do extraordinary things in the lives of his daughters. But here's the catch. God *does* need every woman's permission. Therefore, women must be willing to come into agreement with God to experience his unique plan for each one of them. We must believe what the Bible says about who God is and what he is capable of doing for us, in us, and through us. God wants to be believed, and he wants to be trusted. Once we are willing to believe and trust in him, we become better able to see his glorious plan manifest. It also allows us to experience the truth of his word in operation in our lives. Let's look at the life-changing effect of one serendipitous encounter with Jesus from the story of the Samaritan woman in John 4:5–14 (NKJV). May your faith be strengthened even more as you read this:

> So He came to a city of Samaria which is called Sychar, near the plot of ground that Jacob gave to his son Joseph. Now Jacob's well was there. Jesus therefore, being wearied from His journey, sat thus by the well. It was about the sixth hour. A woman of Samaria came to draw water. Jesus said to her, "Give Me a drink." For His disciples had gone away into the city to buy food. Then the woman of Samaria said to Him, "How is it that You, being a Jew, ask a drink from me, a Samaritan woman?" For Jews have no dealings with Samaritans. Jesus answered and said to her, "If you knew the gift of God, and who it is who says to you, 'Give Me a drink,' you would have asked Him, and He would

have given you living water." The woman said to
Him, "Sir, You have nothing to draw with, and
the well is deep. Where then do You get that living
water? Are You greater than our father Jacob, who
gave us the well, and drank from it himself, as
well as his sons and his livestock?" Jesus answered
and said to her, "Whoever drinks of this water will
thirst again, but whoever drinks of the water that I
shall give him will never thirst. But the water that
I shall give him will become in him a fountain of
water springing up into everlasting life."

John 4:1–42 is a remarkable passage of scripture because
Jesus dispels every reason why women are not called to speak,
lead, and minister. Here are just a few nuggets that I've gleaned
from Jesus's meeting with the Samaritan woman:

1. She was a woman of Samaria. Additionally, she was a
   woman who belonged to a people that were considered
   inferior. Samaritans and Jews hated one another.
2. She had a bad reputation and was isolated from the
   community. Even though she was the "wrong kind of
   woman," Jesus completely ignored this and gave her his
   undivided time and attention.
3. She felt unworthy. When Jesus spoke encouragingly to her,
   she felt it necessary to remind him of her insignificance.
   She was taught and therefore believed what her culture,
   customs, and religious leaders told her about her limitations.
4. Jesus's power was magnified *above* her human condition.
   Jesus taught her that by understanding and accepting who *he*
   was, he could give her everything she needed to be satisfied.
   Ultimately, in the grand scheme of things, it was her cultural
   restrictions that were really insignificant, not her.
5. She questioned Jesus's abilities and doubted that he was
   powerful enough to override her human condition. She
   couldn't see beyond her reality (a false truth).

6. Jesus knew he could change her life *if* she allowed him. He could quench every thirst, meet every need, fulfill every dream.

The passage gets even better. The more the Samaritan woman listened to Jesus, the more she began to believe him! He told her everything that had gone wrong in her life, and he didn't hold it against her. Woman, yes. Disrespected, yes. Bad reputation, yes. Multiple failed relationships, yes. Chosen by God, yes! Made whole, yes! Used in ministry, yes, yes, yes!

Once the woman finally saw herself through Jesus's eyes, she forgot all about her limitations, insignificance, and cultural oppression, which had held her back for years! By simply being in *his* presence, the Samaritan woman ultimately realized she was a winner! She had found someone who believed in her and who called her worthy! This is so powerful! The redeeming power of Jesus can meet you wherever you are! This woman became alive and invigorated after her encounter with Jesus, and he wants to do the same for you! John 4:28–29 tells what she did next:

> The woman then left her water pot, went her way into the city, and said to the men, "Come, see a Man who told me all things that I ever did. Could this be the Christ?" Then they went out of the city and came to Him.

This was a bold move by the Samaritan woman. After being with Jesus, she completely forgot that she was supposed to be ministry-restricted and gender-inferior. She immediately went back to her community and began to evangelize—to the men! Wow! After Jesus revealed to her who she was *in him*, she began operating in her calling! The effectiveness of the Samaritan woman's ministry was evident immediately in John 4:39–42 (NKJV):

> And many of the Samaritans of that city believed in Him because of the word of the woman who testified, "He told me all that I ever did." So when the Samaritans had come to Him, they urged Him

to stay with them; and He stayed there two days. And many more believed because of His own word. Then they said to the woman, "Now we believe, not because of what you said for we ourselves have heard Him and we know that this is indeed the Christ, the Savior of the world."

Here's the lesson. You must learn to be comfortable knowing that not everyone in church or in your family is going to support the calling on your life. Go anyway! Do it anyway! Serve God anyway! Remember, Jesus is with you, and he believes in you. Let your results speak for themselves. God believes in demonstrating that his power is at work within you. He *can* and he *will* use you to show forth his glory.

The Woman Is an Essential Component

I'm reminded of a story I read some years ago told by Loren Cunningham.[1] He's founder of Youth With A Mission and the University of the Nations. The story is about one of the largest churches in the world run by Dr. David Yonggi Cho in Seoul, Korea, and the demonstration of God's power at work through the women in his church. I'm sharing Loren's words here:

> When I first went to Korea thirty years ago, his church was a struggling pioneer work of "only" six thousand. Now Dr. Cho has 763,000 members in his church. Much has been written about the phenomenal growth of this church, but one secret has been overlooked ... Thirty years ago when we were seated in his office, Dr. Cho said, "Loren, I have a problem. My mother-in-law, Mrs. Choi, is an outstanding Bible teacher and preacher. But in our culture, we can't have her teach or preach. What should I do?" I said, "Put her in your pulpit!" He cringed. "Loren, as an American, you don't understand what that means to a Korean!" "Okay,

I have an idea. Get my mom over here to preach for you ..." "Since my mom is from another culture, they'll accept her preaching." I said. "Then as soon as she finishes, put Mrs. Choi in your pulpit. Your people will see the connection. They'll see it isn't a matter of culture but a matter of ministry." Dr. Cho did invite my mother to preach in his church. Following Mom's visit, Mrs. Choi emerged as an outstanding leader and preacher. She was the first of thousands of women who became ministers under Dr. Cho's leadership. Several years later I saw him at a large event ... He told me about a certain country he had just visited where the work of God has struggled for many years. He said, "All their churches are so little! And all of them are holding back their women, not allowing them to do what God calls them to do. I've told them to release their women, but they insist that's not the problem. They ask me, "What's the key to your church?" I tell them again, 'Release your women' but they just don't hear me!" God has given this man the largest church on earth to pastor. He has seven hundred pastors on his staff, including many women. He also has thirty thousand cell groups; the vast majority of these are led by women. Do you think God might be trying to tell all of us something?

Church leaders cannot change what they do not first acknowledge. How can a church know whether or not its low attendance, irrelevance in the community, disenfranchised members, and stagnant church growth are not connected to its resistance to fully utilize women in their ministry callings, if the pastor refuses to have the conversation about how best to incorporate women in church leadership? God created women to coreign, corule, and colead (Genesis 1:26–28). Our denial of this truth does not change the facts. Our denial just keeps us from experiencing all the benefits God had in mind as he envisioned men and women complementing one another in the family, church, community, marketplace and throughout the world!

Men and women of the faith should not allow themselves to be instruments of exploitation and division. We have an enemy for that. Let us remove the works of the enemy from within our ranks so we can defeat his works together by functioning in our respective positions on the same team! We should be unified with singleness of heart and mind toward a common mission to build God's kingdom here on earth. I believe this is God's design for us, and therefore, it can certainly be our new reality. Again, God is looking for those who will choose to cooperate with *his* plan and forgo their own.

As you make the hard decision to carry out your calling and to unapologetically serve God in ministry, learn to accept the fact that people will constantly remind you of why you are not permitted or qualified to speak and teach on behalf of God. Even if you are successfully and competently doing so already, the naysayers, the accusers, and the haters will make their dissatisfaction known. You have to say, so what! You can't focus on the hatred. It's bad enough that you have to wrestle with your own self-defeating thoughts about your capabilities, without feeling a need to prove to others that God has placed this gift in you that you must fulfill.

Unfortunately, you will eventually have to contend with these external forces at work to stop you, but don't fret, you can prevail. My philosophy to combat such external chatter is to do what Jesus did against Satan. In Luke 4:1–13, Jesus was in the wilderness dealing with the enemy, and he did it masterfully. I call it the, "It is Also Written Approach." Every time Satan met Jesus with a perverted, misrepresentation of a scripture from the Bible meant to put darkness at an advantage, Jesus immediately countered, "It is also written," and knocked the wind out of Satan's twisted interpretation. This is important to note because although Satan was giving accurate scripture, it was erroneously interpreted and applied. You must remember that the *whole* Bible has been given to us for doctrine, correction, and guidance for righteous living (2 Timothy 3:16–17). Learn what the Bible says for yourself, so you are always ready to defend your faith and your position in Christ (1 Peter 3:15).

Other Elephants

There are other elephants that have entered the church that we must also confront: racism, homosexuality, and mental health. To be successful in giving ample attention to these delicate and important issues, we desperately need women leaders in position to assist. Men are ill-equipped to face these growing issues without the experience, wisdom, emotional support, sensitivity, discernment, compassion, and leadership of capable, competent women. I believe the lack of adequate representation of women in positions of authority and responsibility in establishing the direction of our churches is proving fatal for our men pastors. Pastors are overwhelmed, and they are struggling with their own personal and family issues, mental illness, and burnout. The percentages of suicide and divorce are growing within this population as well.

Men are carrying more than they should, they are not getting ample support, and they are failing at administering adequate self-care to shield themselves from self-destructive behaviors. Do we truly believe this is what God intended for the church and for our men? Often times, male pastors live isolated lives. It was this isolation that caused God to send man a suitable companion that could help him govern the earth. Here are some sobering statistics[2] that demonstrate the increasing struggles of clergy:

➤ 80 percent believe pastoral ministry has negatively affected their families. Many pastors' children do not attend church now because of what the church has done to their parents.

➤ 53 percent of pastors report that the seminary did not prepare them for the ministry.

➤ 57 percent of pastors are unable to pay their bills.

➤ 80 percent of pastors and 84 percent of their spouses have felt unqualified and discouraged in their role of pastors at least one or more times in their ministry.

➤ 52 percent of pastors feel overworked and cannot meet their church's unrealistic expectations.

➤ 54 percent of pastors find the role of a pastor overwhelming.

➤ 80 percent of pastors expect conflict within their church.

> ➤ 35 percent of pastors battle depression or fear of inadequacy.
> ➤ 28 percent of pastors report they are spiritually undernourished.
> ➤ 70 percent of pastors report they have a lower self-image now than when they first started.
> ➤ 70 percent of pastors do *not* have someone they consider to be a close friend.
> ➤ 57 percent of pastors feel fulfilled but yet discouraged, stressed, and fatigued.
> ➤ 84 percent of pastors desire to have close fellowship with someone they can trust and confide with.
> ➤ Over 50 percent of pastors are unhealthy and overweight and do not exercise.
> ➤ The profession of pastor is near the bottom of a survey of the most-respected professions, just above car salesman.
> ➤ Many denominations are reporting an empty pulpit crisis. They do not have a shortage of ministers but have a shortage of ministers desiring to fill the role of a pastor.

If we want better results within our churches, we must be willing to change. That change starts with us acknowledging the challenges that need tackling. Then we need to acknowledge, by God's design, that both men and women belong in leadership roles, working together, for the edification of the saints, and the advancement of the kingdom (1 Corinthians 11:11; Ephesians 4:11). This is the way we can best undergird and oversee our beloved churches.

According to scripture, and the full counsel of the word of God, we are admonished to allow every joint in the body of Christ to function as God created us to do, not saying to anyone that they're not needed (Ephesians 4:16), because they are. Mark my word. As long as women are not in place, we will only see the results of what men are able to accomplish as they strive in their own natural strength making up only half of God's abilities. We hold God hostage and unable to do any sustained miracles among us because we don't believe that his plan for men and women coleading and coreigning, is viable.

Based on the statistics above, we can see that our church

organizations and church leadership structures, in their current state, are not operating effectively or victoriously. Clearly, this is not a positive representation of the God of the universe and is a poor reflection of his holy name. Yet, I am not dismayed. We're still in this together. God is depending on us to figure this mess out. Let's roll up our sleeves and get busy. Before we get started, can we first admit that we can't afford to operate the same way as in the past? Is it apparent that the rules of engagement must change to meet the current demands facing our churches? Working together is the only kingdom answer that will yield the results we desire. And working together is the only way to get these elephants out of our churches!

Chapter 10

The R.E.F.R.E.S.H.® Model

A Collective Response

*A*s an ordained pastor and a practitioner in the field of conflict resolution, I have had to make a careful yet intentional decision to marry together my spiritual and intellectual beliefs to meet the needs of people—spirit, soul, and body. I have endeavored through this book to provide a balanced look at the issue of gender discrimination in the church by offering information gained through Bible study, academic research, and personal experience. My summation is this: to meet the growing need of confronting the long-standing gender conflict still prevalent in today's churches, it will require more than prayer. To see effective change, our prayers will need to be coupled with a renewed mind, a deeper love for others, and a commitment to take the necessary actions to realize the desired unity and power that our churches are capable of harnessing.

Introducing Critical Pedagogy

As a conflict coach and resolutionist, it is my professional recommendation that church leaders in greater numbers commit to unlearn subjective concepts, dogma, or traditions that just aren't working *for* their congregants. Then they should acquire knowledge to obtain objective godly concepts, dogma, and traditions that ensure positive and advancing changes relevant to inspiring increased enthusiasm *from* their congregants. To do this will take courage and a resolve that church transformation as it relates to the utilization of women is now a requirement and no longer an option. In determining the best approach to help churches become places of empowerment and healthy growth, it has been through my study of philosopher and educator Paulo Freire that I have concluded what it will take to accomplish these goals.

As reported in my research, Paulo Freire[1] developed the concept of critical pedagogy of the oppressed (or critical education/teaching of oppression) after extensive observation of an indigenous society economically and educationally disadvantaged by the wealthy and powerful. The premise of critical pedagogy of oppression is that oppression exists, and the only way people can free themselves from oppression is through the education of transformation. He defined oppression as "any instance in which 'A' objectively exploits 'B' or hinders self-affirmation."[2]

Freire also mentioned that it is systematic, that even the oppressor is not aware that he or she is engaging in the oppression. What is important to note is that although it is the oppressor who appears to have the ability to liberate the oppressed, it is only through the empowerment of the oppressed that both the oppressed and the oppressor can ultimately and permanently be made free. Through training and experimentations, Freire learned that people possessed a "fear of freedom," which he clarified to be not just a fear of freedom, but the fear of the risk associated with freedom. Freire argued that men and women who have been oppressed might not be conscious of injustice or oppression in any given situation. [3] For one to be liberated, critical consciousness and education about one's condition are necessary. He stated,

> The oppressed suffer from the duality which has established itself in their innermost being. They discover that without freedom they cannot exist authentically. Yet, although they desire authentic

existence, they fear it. They are at one and the same time themselves and the oppressor whose consciousness they have internalized. The conflict lies in the choice between being wholly themselves or being divided; between ejecting the oppressor within or not ejecting them; between human solidarity or alienation; between following prescriptions or having choices; between being spectators or actors; between acting or having the illusion of acting through the action of the oppressors; between speaking out or being silent, castrated in their power to create and re-create, in their power to transform the world. This is the tragic dilemma of the oppressed which their education must take into account.[4]

This type of critical consciousness requires what Freire terms "praxis," which is reflection, critical dialogue, and then action. All three elements must be involved for the oppressed to experience self-affirmation and liberation. Freire says *critical reflection* is deep contemplation on the conditions of those oppressed: looking at their plight and coming to conclusions about steps that need to occur to rectify their situation. *Critical dialogue* entails open and genuinely transparent communication about the oppressive conditions where trust and honesty prevail. The oppressor must provide an opportunity to hear and discuss what the oppressed have experienced in their situation. Praxis also requires *action*, which means intentional steps taken to change. The goals of critical pedagogy are to determine the cause of oppression, then to address the subjective nature of oppression through "objective transformation of reality."[5] This process liberates the oppressed from stagnation at the individual level, allowing for renewed awareness leading to positive and forward-thinking change.

The Destabilization of the Patriarchal System

Despite best efforts by both men and women, the patriarchal system still plays a significant role in hampering female clergy leaders from achieving success. This is consistent with past research findings. Sociologist Cecilia Ridgeway linked the church as a symbolic representation of male patriarchy and power. [6] This image has not changed despite the increase in clergywomen over the recent decades. Men have traditionally benefited from this practice. Now, more than ever, women clergy leaders threaten to destabilize this phenomenon. Participants in my research found this type of behavior to be best defined as either discriminatory or biased against women. Therefore, praxis through critical pedagogy is essential for religious organizations to transform their toxic practices against the advancement of female leaders.

Empowering Churches and Women via the R.E.F.R.E.S.H.® Model

To empower women, improved consciousness is necessary. Critical pedagogy is a way of learning that helps to liberate people from oppression.[7] It suggests the dawning of a new era of equality; the establishment of new social norms; and the welcoming of new ideas, operations, and inclusion of both men and women at the highest levels within our churches.

As cofounder of Empower to Engage, a coaching and consulting firm, I have worked closely with church leaders to accomplish two primary goals: (1) transforming their operational focus by helping them deeply consider the needs of the members, spiritually and personally, and (2) enhancing their interactions with church staff and members through the development of conflict resolution and conflict management techniques. We accomplish this mission by utilizing our R.E.F.R.E.S.H.® management techniques, which represent the core values we endeavor to model:

- **Refine:** Refine values, goals, and vision as needed to establish organizational change that promotes a healthy work culture and environment.
- **Explore:** Explore new methodologies annually that may increase job satisfaction at every level to sustain organizational vitality.

- **Focus:** Focus on the needs of the employees and leaders equally—always with integrity and respect.
- **Redesign:** Redesign organizational practices that reduce the value or benefits of our key stakeholders: our employees (ministerial staff in the case of church organizations).
- **Exercise:** Exercise free-flowing communication at every level of the organization, and reward creativity and innovation.
- **Structure:** Structure the evaluation of conflict prevention methods and training implementations of all newly incorporated organizational systems; evaluation is key.
- **Help**: Help stakeholders actualize their maximum potential for promotion and job satisfaction (ordination in the case of church organizations).

As an organizational conflict management analyst, I firmly believe every organization intent on discarding practices that disenfranchise women from authentically engaging in leadership can R.E.F.R.E.S.H.® their current ways of doing business and ministry. These changes can occur both internally and externally by having a comprehensive and collective response to handling conflicting interests at every level. As with any new ideology, steps must be put into place to R.E.F.R.E.S.H.® old ways of thinking that hinder effective progress. Above all else, be determined to usher in a new mindset that is beneficial not to a specific few, but to all members of the organization who have an equal stake in its success—and that means wholeheartedly including women as voting, empowered, and ordained leaders.

Chapter 11

Where Can We Go from Here?

The Future of "Ministry" Has No Limits

Ministry in the Church—What Can We Expect?

*T*he twenty-first century marks a historic movement for women and women leaders. Although it may be difficult and may take years to finally make the decision, possibly causing alienation and broken relationships, female church leaders are increasingly breaking with the traditional patriarchal system. We must remember that in some regard, women defy conventional wisdom by even considering the path of the clergy. The cost to them to do so is often at great personal and emotional peril. Many express uncertainty and tension related to serving in leadership positions. Logically they know that they are capable of leading, but they still feel inadequate based on toxic church practices against their advancement.

However, the tolerance level of such gendered rejection of women is waning. Women are becoming tired and apathetic, choosing to just quit altogether, even though the calling and the fire to serve still burns on the inside of them. In reviewing the data and hearing the stories of the research participants, it's hard to imagine that this is what God intended when he fashioned the beauty of Eve in the garden and made her Adam's helper, as well as a source of strength, wisdom, and authority, comparable to him. She was expected to stand alongside him as a ruler over all the earth. This has not been happening to the magnitude that it should.

The argument about gender inequality in churches is not just about competency or competition. It is also about the fact that women are running into barriers of acceptance. Church members can be outright mean and disrespectful to women who pursue clergy positions. This behavior needs to be discussed and then corrected. For women, it can impede their sense of identity. It can also have them confused and questioning how best to serve God when they deeply and desperately want to please the very people who dissuade them from pursuing their ministry aspirations. Societal norms are changing. We need a compassionate and sweeping shift in our religious institutions for both the historically oppressed (women) and the intended/unintended oppressors (men).

We as women solicit a new stage of consciousness—a critical and deliberate consciousness. As shared throughout this book, the women in my study confessed to feeling stuck, stifled, disregarded, and rejected at various times during their involvement in the church. Since the writing of this book, I know of one of the women participants who has walked away from her church duties. This is because, as research revealed, women's success has been contingent on the support and encouragement of her fellow churchgoers.[1] Women desire this support even though many church leaders have no plans to ever ordain or promote them, regardless of their stellar and committed church service.

Participants from my study expressed mixed feedback from others, be it church or family members, as they climbed the ecclesiastical ladder. Some shared occurrences of members being malicious and disapproving of their decision to accept leadership positions causing them to continuously question or second guess themselves. They simply did not want to be alienated. Other participants expressed a sense of comradery and praise from others for achieving such accomplishments. Whatever the response, there has been no continuity in what women can expect to hear. It is important for men church leaders to understand that the health, supportive nature, and gender-neutral developmental objectivity offered to women by their churches is a direct reflection on that leader, the church culture, and his ability to lead well or not. Patriarchal responses to instances of gender bias, discrimination, and misogynistic behavior will determine the longevity and strength of a predominantly male-led church. Let this be a warning.

The calling of God is a kingdom calling, not a church calling. This means that people can use their gifts wherever they live, work, and play, not only where they worship. To prepare Christians to serve God in this manner, *empowerment* through education beginning at the local church is where the preparation should begin. So what exactly would it mean to empower women, and what would it look like? Dr. Cindy Trimm,[2] speaker and author, offers the most comprehensive definition and description of empowerment, which can provide some direction:

> The definition of empowerment is the process by which an individual or a group of individuals are assisted, equipped, strengthened in order for them to discover their potential, identify their capabilities, access available resources, while at the same time, enabling them to identify, exploit and leverage opportunities, in order to maximize their own strength and potential, hone their own skills and abilities, become self-sufficient and think at a higher or more advanced level, for the fulfillment of an aim, an objective, a goal or a purpose. This is all so that they can ultimately be led into sustainable wealth, fulfillment, success, prosperity, and happiness. So the message of the Kingdom is a message of empowerment.

If churches are not empowering women to apply their best attributes (through their gifts, callings, abilities), it is reasonably assumed, based on the research data, that the contrary is occurring. Moreover, if any church is not empowering women, but instead demonstrates a willingness to restrict a woman's ability to grow, teach, lead, or speak disregarding her desired effort to serve God, or refuses to submit to a woman's authority when she has been duly ordained to serve as clergy, it means that they, in no uncertain terms, believe that God does not know what he's doing. Such people have therefore closed their hearts, minds, and spirits from receiving direction or guidance through a vessel of God's choosing. That's dangerous ground to tread, and it hinders expectations of growth, commitment, and the development of healthy relationships, which are all needed for a church to flourish.

Ministry in the Marketplace— What Can We Envision?

We discussed in chapter 3 that the percentage of women in the workforce has reached 57.1 percent. That's over half of the population! Additionally, women own almost 10 million businesses in the United States. [3] It's certain that women are vital contributors to the stability and success of both secular and religious organizations. These numbers don't even reflect the global presence of women. Can you imagine if we still thought, as a society, that women should remain barefoot and pregnant? Try to imagine the many spiritual, scientific, medical, technological, relational, and educational advances America would have forfeited had women been denied full expression of their capabilities. Imagine if the Bible offered no examples of the wonders of women and how they too have helped shape our faith. I shudder to think about it.

My scholarly research and this book present an opportunity for us all to *investigate* what ministry and leadership might look like for women beyond ministry exclusively or primarily within religious organizations, namely churches. This research can be used to critically conceptualize the notion that women who are working in the marketplace can accept nonchurch opportunities as ways to garner true fulfillment and function as rewarding ministry opportunities to serve God. Ministry can occur through your work in areas such as business/economics, media, education, arts/entertainment, government/law, or family. This line of thinking is evolutionary, imaginative, limitless, and freeing!

Here is something else to consider as we move forward. Although the data collected in my research supports the need for increasing women leadership within our churches, another goal of this work is to *substantiate* why women need to consider leadership and ministry *outside* of the church. This book provides additional weight, proof, and significance to demonstrate women's contributions in marketplace ministry and to encourage women to seek a sense of purpose beyond what they may believe can only come through service within a church organization. The sole basis for this argument is to champion a woman's right to fully respond to God's call to serve him in ministry, no matter how or where she does it.

Since churches continue to disregard women, a broader definition of ministry is needed to allow women to experience a fulfilled and rewarding life. We have not fully grasped that we *the people* are the church. *We. Are. The. Church* (1 Corinthians 3:16 NIV). No matter where we go, we take Christ and the kingdom with us, and we should all do our best to represent kingdom principles and serve as ministers of reconciliation as we have been mandated to do in scripture (2 Corinthians 5:16–21). We can accomplish this through all types of opportunities presented to us. My prayer is that women will walk and live in the freedom for which Christ has already made us free (Galatians 5:1). If we choose to do this, women can experience ministry expressed in various creative and rewarding ways. Just let your imaginations soar!

A Woman's Declaration to the Church

Of the research participants I spoke with, there was one woman whose words seemed prophetic, having a profound impact on me. I believe she was used by God during her interview to confirm to me that this book was not my idea but *his* and that this book will prove essential to women everywhere who are determined to advance beyond their current position in life and ministry.

Elder Diane's experiences and candid forewarning regarding the state of churches standing against women should be heeded as a likely outcome if pastors choose to ignore the compelling signs of the deteriorating patriarchal leadership-dominating church model. Those individuals or churches who refuse to embrace the need for organizational change stand to be credibly identified as likely forces against the advancement of the church (Matthew 12:25–30). Such a choice to ignore the cries, pleas, and anguish of women, and to continue refusing to embrace and acknowledge their leadership ability, denies called women who have been faithful, integral, and available a freedom that Jesus died for them to have. Let's consider Diane's insight that follows.

Coming to a place of trusting God was a long, painful road for Diane. In her early years, she considered herself a churchgoer and the kid of a minister. But she never really thought of herself as a Christian. During Diane's formative years, she did not see many women leaders in the church. However, as the years progressed, she marveled that, "I've seen women move from the pew to the pulpit." Diane had never wrestled with the idea of whether women should be in leadership. In her mind, God could use whomever he pleased. Since Diane had been busy doing the work of church ministry for so many years, the barriers for women in ministry had a small degree of impact on her. However, the sobering reality of the disparate treatment came across clearly when she asserted,

> I'm finding that even as women make certain advances within the church, there are still barriers there, and sometimes they come from other women. There are still barriers there that it's difficult to get through. There are still, if I can put it using a secular description here, there's still a certain glass ceiling that's there. There's still a pecking order that's there. And you deal with the ministry but then you have to deal with the politics of that environment that you're in and you have to be—you have to sometimes be aware of the fact that people still have you in—well they want to have you in a place.

Diane expressed concerns for the generations to come if there is no change in how women are handled in the church, and, if there is no concerted effort to accurately educate people regarding what the Bible says about women and their identity in God. According to Diane, new women leaders need proper training to do the work of ministry instead of just being thrown into positions without proper guidance. She warned,

> And that's another issue, we have become church members. Okay. And there's a difference between being a church member and being someone who recognizes that you are part of a kingdom and part of a lifestyle and that lifestyle impacts not only what happens in here [church building], it impacts what happens in your home and that impacts what happens out in the marketplace, as you use that terminology. So that's what we've got to get back to. And the time is very short. It is very short. And I'm—I'll say this one last thing: I'm afraid in America if the church does not wake up soon, it may be too late.[4]

Diane has given us a chilling message. The bright light at the end of the tunnel for it is this: women have options. In fact, women's ability to serve beyond the church walls can be scripturally supported with Jesus's great commission. He told his followers to go out into all the world to preach the gospel (Mark 16:15–18). In fact, we have been directed to be salt and light in the world (Matthew 5:13–16). Did these commands ever change? The answer is emphatically, no. The Bible teaches that Jesus saw the work of ministry extending to the ends of the world. When Jesus gave this instruction, women were included in receiving that charge (Acts 1:1–14).

Remember, it is up to you to seek God to discover what part of the world *you* are called to service with the ministry gifts you possess. To this very day, all the world still needs ministry from women. Believe it or not, every woman is the answer to somebody's prayer. We don't need a church pastor, male or female, to give us permission to be a blessing to others. No person should have the right to tell you to go be great. You must settle this matter in your heart and mind because it's already settled with God.

Final Charge to Eve

The mandate given to Eve resides in every woman, everywhere, without exception. You, woman, bear the responsibility to respond to God's call on your life. The discovery and the execution of his will for your life lays squarely on your shoulders. Should you choose not to give your life in service to God's purpose, there is no one to blame but yourself. We have all been offered an awesome opportunity to make a difference in this world. God chose you as the best person to impact the sphere of influence he has designated to you. It's why you were born. It's precisely why you're here! The story behind your birth or your past mistakes do not matter (just like the Samaritan woman in John 4). The *call* on your life is not affected by any of these things.

In the beginning and middle of this book I posed several questions to you, and I'll ask them here once again. Now is the time, with deep reflection, for you to do your level best to answer them. What do you do when you, (1) have a passion or a sense of duty to *be* something or to *do* something that may be contrary to what others think is right for you (those others could be a boss, coworker, business partner, family member, professor, pastor, friend, or even your spouse); (2) have a burden to go after a skill, a vocation, a career, a business, or anything else that you have been taught is flat out wrong for you to have—so it causes you to doubt yourself; or (3) believe in your heart that you have been born to pursue a cause beyond your capacity or current abilities? Now, I have another question to ask: What do you do when you don't feel that God has any real purpose for your life or you've chosen to believe the lie that you can't make a real difference because you don't feel like a leader? If you still find it difficult to answer any of these questions, I'll give you one final Bible account to encourage you to take the leap.

The book of Esther in the Bible highlights the stories of two very different women: Vashti, the outgoing queen, and Esther, the incoming queen. Both women's stories are important. At various points in our lives we may find ourselves in either one of the situations presented by each woman. Vashti, already in a place of prominence as queen, seemed to understand her worth based on her actions. Her willingness to deny the king's request to see her demonstrated that she no longer cared what others thought of the choices she felt she had to make for her own well-being. Vashti wanted to be respected and valued. She felt responding to the king's request to parade her beauty in front of his guests was disrespectful and degrading. Perhaps in the past she had accepted such requests when she was insecure and a people-pleaser. That's my assessment of the situation. However, in this story, Queen Vashti was now at a point in her life where she needed and therefore demanded more from those around her, including the king.

Esther, on the other hand, was just beginning to learn her worth. Since she lacked confidence when she was selected as the new queen, she often acquiesced to whatever she was told to do. She was careful to stay in her place unless the king or other officials told her otherwise. When there came a time for her to exercise authority as the new queen, she was fearful to challenge any of the king's decrees. She didn't grasp the magnitude of the responsibility that came along with her God-given assignment. When Esther failed to respond as expected to a crisis, her cousin, who raised her like a daughter, gave her a wake-up call. He told her she was in her position as queen for the very purpose of saving her nation, the Jews. Unbeknownst to her, she was strategically positioned to act in a manner that would save their very lives, all by God's design!

Both women had to search deep within themselves to find the strength they needed to take action. Both women ultimately made decisions that took great bravery. And both women's stories can teach us how to stand in times of pressure or adversity. These women speak to us to do two things as we mature throughout life: (1) remind ourselves of our worth and (2) reevaluate our involvement with any situation that makes us feel that our worth is being compromised. You must assess whether the methods you employ to fit in, be liked, or not appear "difficult" are helping or hindering your personal, professional, or spiritual progress. Based on your answers, you may conclude that those methods are not going to work for you anymore. Own that. You may realize that you've undermined your own abilities just to appease someone else. Perhaps you finally realize you've been doubting yourself, and you're capable of doing so much more! Go ahead, celebrate that.

It's possible to not realize the significance of your role in any particular situation that you find yourself in. Nonetheless, it doesn't change the reason why you're there. There are a people, a circumstance, a cause that you have been called to change. And like Eve, Queen Vashti, Esther, and any other woman you know who is living and conducting herself like a boss, you have been equipped to serve at the highest levels both in the church and in the marketplace. This also calls for a celebration! God truly has a plan for your life too! Give yourself permission to believe that!

> For we are His workmanship [His own master work, a work of art], created in Christ Jesus [reborn from above—spiritually transformed, renewed, ready to be used] for good works, which God prepared [for us] beforehand [taking paths which He set], so that we would walk in them [living the good life which He prearranged and made ready for us]. (Ephesians 2:10 AMP)

Never forget, it all started with Eve. She, along with Adam, was given the command to rule and have dominion in the earth. The moment is now upon you, and the day has arrived! It's time to take your position. Come forward and step into the light. Everyone needs to see you. So when the question is asked, "Eve, where are you?" you can confidently say, "I'm here!"

Special Note

On the weekend I drafted the final chapter of this book, I was notified that Saturday evening by text to tune into the upcoming Sunday service for the church I used to attend. This church and pastor were the catalyst used by God to show me my expanded ministry to women. I was told that by watching the service, "You and your ministry will be greatly encouraged." I eagerly obliged and watched the first of three church services offered online, Sunday, January 26, 2020, at 8:00 a.m.

Much to my amazement and complete joy, *the* pastor, who (1) I spoke with and shared my heart about women and the need for ordained women leaders; (2) shared books with me for my doctoral dissertation that characterized justifications for the role of women; (3) knew of the struggles, frustrations, and resistance I had experienced as the director of the women's ministry within his church; and (4) recognized mine and other women's gifts, skills, and abilities, but found no scriptural allowance to ordain women to senior positions within his church, made a decision that will forever change the landscape of his church.

With a newfound conviction after pastoring his church for twenty-eight years, this pastor publicly ordained the first woman pastor in the history of the church! Finally! Standing before a congregation of thousands of people, he admitted that he was wrong about the role of women! It was a glorious and victorious moment! I cried. I cried for him, I cried for the woman who was being ordained, I cried for other women who were watching, hoping … and … I cried … for me.

The timing of this momentous event and the confirming realization of the truth of God's plan for me is extremely reassuring.

It validates that I *was* hearing from God about the value and significance of his women in the earth the whole time. On that fateful Sunday while talking with my son, so many years ago, when I sensed God's leading to care about women, I hesitantly started this good work from sheer obedience to God's voice deep in my heart. Now I confidently partner with God to advance his kingdom for the upbuilding and edification of his glorious church—the bride of Christ—and it feels so good! Onward and upward!

Empower to Engage Coaching and Consulting Firm

EMP⏻WER TO ENGAGE

The R.E.F.R.E.S.H.® Conflict Management Philosophy

The R.E.F.R.E.S.H.® Model aids in stressing the importance of both education and implementation of learned information. This dual perspective provides opportunities for church leaders and members to gain understanding about the impacts of disparate treatment toward women as outlined in this book, and it incorporates the necessary steps to address these issues as it pertains to the individuals and the systems governing them. Both the men and women research participants gave a plethora of examples of the changes needed within their churches to forge ahead as relevant examples in society as suggested and intended by the doctrines and tenants of the Christian faith.

Our R.E.F.R.E.S.H.® approach to rebuilding management systems is a threefold system design addressing deficiencies in the following areas: organizational development, relationship development, and leadership development. Our threefold system is a customized program designed specifically to meet the unique needs of each client through consultation and coaching, education and training, and assessments and evaluations. Churches can benefit from these services as well. We recognize churches as organizations that are made up of people working toward a common goal, vision, and mission. This program model can be used to assist church leaders who desire to modify current practices by utilizing our step-by-step system. This model has been developed to target, address, and eliminate barriers to growth in various areas including hiring, promotion and ordination practices, toxic work and religious cultural dynamics, and resistance to change factors.

To solidify our commitment to fostering unity within organizations, we subscribe to the *Ubuntu* message of the native South African people who live below the Sahara. It is the message that every person *is* because someone else is.[1] We believe in the value of others and strive to demonstrate this belief by recognizing what every person brings to an organization through the evaluation of their skills and the solicitation of their perspectives. Conflict can be diminished by better managing the way we connect and communicate with every person around us. We believe, and therefore we teach, that our interactions with others should be positive, empowering, and constructive.

For churches that are interested in utilizing our R.E.F.R.E.S.H.® model to transform their current business and ministry practices, or would like more information about these services, visit our website at <u>www.empowertoengage.com</u>.

About the Author

Nicole L. Davis, PhD

Dr. Nicole Davis has a passion for family, women, and leadership development that has evolved and strengthened over many decades. As a wife of almost three decades and the mother of two adult sons, family enrichment has been her number-one priority. Her passion for the topic of *leadership* started during her years in the US Navy. From there, she has provided education and training to leaders in several arenas and on various levels, including nonprofits, government, corporations, collegiate, and church.

Dr. Davis's doctorate from Nova Southeastern University, Ft. Lauderdale, Florida, is in the field of conflict analysis and resolution, with an emphasis in organizational conflict. She also holds a master's degree in international management from the University of Maryland and a bachelor's degree in social work from Morgan State University. She is a certified mediator, facilitator, conflict coach and Christian life coach, and a certified marriage trainer.

As a marketplace leader, Dr. Davis has been employed by various governmental agencies. And as a church leader, Dr. Davis has served in multiple capacities to strengthen and develop ministries and programs. She has gained affection from couples, women, and leaders for her teaching and leadership style for being caring, firm, but fair.

Along with her husband, Tony, she has coauthored multiple books. First they wrote the three-book *Done Right* series, which includes: *Parenting Done Right Is Hard Work (But It's Worth It!); Marriage Done Right Is Hard Work (But It's Work It!)*; and

Leadership Done Right Is Hard Work (But It's Worth It!). These books bring voice to what God is speaking regarding family dynamics and the conduct of the individuals within them. The couple also coauthored the anthology *Speak to the Mountains!* Later, Dr. Davis went on to write for the anthology *Junia Arise: Apostolic Women on the Frontlines.*

Dr. Davis has cofounded Empower to Engage, an organization that focuses on enhancing marriages, families, and organizations. They equip men, women, and leaders with tools and techniques essential for effective and righteous leadership in their spheres of societal influence. Visit their website: www.empowertoengage.com.

More from
Dr. Nicole L. Davis

Marriage Done Right Is Hard Work (But It's Worth It!)

This thirty-one-day guide shows couples how to get the absolute best out of themselves and their marriage. As easy as it is today to walk away from the marriage covenant, it is actually just as easy to stay *if* we commit to living out marriage God's way.

Parenting Done Right Is Hard Work (But It's Worth It!)

This thirty-one-day guide helps parents navigate the challenging, stressful, yet rewarding role of parenting. It serves as a go-to handbook to help address some of the toughest issues we face in our increasingly not-so-child-friendly world.

Leadership Done Right Is Hard Work (But It's Worth It!)

This thirty-one-day guide challenges every person to lead *themselves* first and provides the strategies to do so. How we make decisions, conduct ourselves, and interact with others are the ultimate tests to our level of success in every area of life. Improving yourself will make you a person that others will want to follow.

To invite Dr. Nicole and/or her and her husband, Tony, to speak at your next event, contact them with details:

Phone: 1-800-345-0805
Email: info@empowertoengage.com

Visit their websites for more information on resources and services.

Website: www.empowertoengage.com
Facebook: www.facebook.com/empowertoengage/

Website: www.evewhereareyou.com
Facebook: www.facebook.com/evewhereareyou/

Endnotes

Chapter 1

1 U.S. Equal Employment of Opportunity Commission. *Title VII of the Civil Rights Act of 1964.* Retrieved from https://www.eeoc.gov/laws/statutes/titlevii.cfm

2 Elwell, W. A., & Elwell, W. A. (1996). *Evangelical dictionary of biblical theology.* Grand Rapids, MI: Baker Book House.

Chapter 2

1 Pew Forum Research (2016, March 22). *The gender gap in religion around the world: Women are generally more religious than men, particularly among Christians.* Retrieved from https://www.pewforum.org/2016/03/22/the-gender-gap-in-religion-around-the-world/

2 Bilezikian, G. (2006). *Beyond sex roles: What the Bible says about a woman's place in church and family.* Grand Rapids, MI: Baker Academic.

3 Piper, J., & Grudem, W. (2006). *Recovering Biblical manhood & womanhood: A response to evangelical feminism.* Wheaton, IL: Crossway.

4 Machen, J.G. (2009). *Christianity and liberalism.* Grand Rapids, MI: Wm B. Eerdmans Publishing.

5 Groothuis, R. M. (1994). *Women caught in the conflict: The culture war between traditionalism and feminism.* Eugene, OR: WIPF & Stock.

Pierce, R. W. & Groothuis, R. M. (2004). *Discovering biblical equality: Complementarity without hierarchy.* Downers Grove, IL: InterVarsity Press Academic.

6   Grudem, W., & Grudem E. (2005). *Christian beliefs.* Grand Rapids, MI: Zondervan

Elwell, W. A., & Elwell, W. A. (1996). *Evangelical dictionary of biblical theology.* Grand Rapids, MI: Baker Book House.

Fairchild, M. (2019, April 17). *Basic beliefs of Christianity. Tenants of Christianity.* Retrieved from https://www.learnreligions.com/basic-christian-beliefs-700357

7   Clouse, B., Clouse, R. G. (1989). *Women in ministry: Four views.* Downers Grove, IL: IVP Academic.

8   Barna Research Group (2012, August 13). *Christian women today part 1 of 4 what women think of faith leadership and their role in the church.* Retrieved from https://www.barna.com/ research/christian-women-today-part-1-of-4-what-women-think-of-faith-leadership-and-their-role-in-the-church/

Chapter 3

1   NASA. (2019, October 17). *Friday's all-woman spacewalk: The basics.* Retrieved from https://www.nasa.gov/feature/fridays-all-woman-spacewalk-the-basics

2   Ridgeway, C. (2009). Framed before we know it: How gender shapes social relations. *Gender & Society - Gender Soc.* 23, 145–60. doi: 10.1177/0891243208330313

3   Barna Research Group (2012, August 13). *Christian women today part 1 of 4 what women think of faith leadership and their role in the church.* Retrieved from https://www.barna.com/ research/christian-women-today-part-1-of-4-what-women-think-of-faith-leadership-and-their-role-in-the-church/

4   Gallagher, S. K. (2003). *Evangelical identity and gendered family life.* New Brunswick, NJ: Rutgers University Press.

5   Capitani, D. (2003). Imagining God in our ways: The journals of Frances E. Willard. *Feminist Theology*,12, 75–88.

6   US Bureau of Labor Statistics (2020, April 21). *Economic news release*. Retrieved from https://www.bls.gov/news.release/famee.nr0.htm

US Bureau of Labor Statistics (2019). *Labor force statistics from the current population survey*. Retrieved from https://www.bls.gov/cps/cpsaat03.htm

7   The Digerati Life. (2007, May 29). Traditional Jobs For Men And Women And The Gender Divide by Silicon Valley Blogger Retrieved from http://www.thedigeratilife.com/blog/index.php/2007/05/29/traditional-jobs-for-men-and-women-the-gender-divide/

8   McKay, D. R. (2019, June 25). *Non-traditional careers for women*. The Balance Careers. Retrieved from https://www.thebalancecareers.com/non-traditional-careers-for-women-525715

9   Bessey, S. (2013). *Jesus feminist: An invitation to revisit the Bible's view of women*. New York: Howard.

10 Trout, L. J. (2014). *A study of attitudes toward women serving in any office if elected by the ministerial constituency of the united pentecostal church international* (Doctoral dissertation). Available from ProQuest Dissertations & Theses Global. (UMI No. 1498130586)

Chapter 4

1   Quote by Edmund Burke.

2   Barnes, S. L. (2006). Whosoever will let her come: Social activism and gender inclusivity in the black church, *Journal for the Scientific study of Religion*, 45 (3), 371–87.

3   Ibid.

4   Suckle, J. A. (2005). Challenges and resolution strategies of ordained protestant clergywomen (Doctoral dissertation). Available from ProQuest Dissertations & Theses Global. (UMI No. 305391776)

Arnold, D. L. W. (2001). *A phenomenological exploration of eight clergywomen's stories through a postmodern lens* (Doctoral dissertation). Available from ProQuest Dissertations & Theses Global. (UMI No. 251758860)

5   Durham, L. (2016, October). *The debate over female leadership in ministry.* Conference Paper. North Carolina Agricultural and Technical State University. Retrieved from https://www. researchgate.net/publication/312167004

6   Pew Forum Research (2016, March 22). The gender gap in religion around the world: Women are generally more religious than men, particularly among Christians. Retrieved from https://www.pewforum. org/2016/03/22/the-gender-gap-in-religion-around-the-world/

7   Groothuis, R. M. (1994). *Women caught in the conflict: The culture war between traditionalism and feminism.* Eugene, OR: WIPF & Stock.

Chapter 5

1   McLeod, S. (2019). Social identity theory. Simply Psychology. Retrieved from https://www.simplypsychology.org/social-identity-theory.html

2   Klenke, K. (2007). Authentic leadership: A self, leader, and spiritual identity perspective. *International Journal of Leadership Studies,* 3(1). 68–97.

3   Lexico Dictionary, Retrieved from www.Lexico.com

4   Erikson, E. H. & Erikson, J. M. (1997) *The Life Cycle Completed: Extended Version.* New York: W. W. Norton

5   Barna Research Group (2012, August 13). *Christian women today part 1 of 4 what women think of faith leadership and their role in the church.* Retrieved from https://www.barna.com/ research/christian-women-today-part-1-of-4-what-women-think-of-faith-leadership-and-their-role-in-the-church/

6   Truman, A. W. (2010). *The lived experience of leadership for female pastors in religious organizations* (Doctoral dissertation). Available from ProQuest Dissertations & Theses Global. (UMI No. 753892386)

Chapter 6

1   Roberts, A. (2003). *Hitler and Churchill: Secrets of leadership.* London: Weidenfeld & Nicolson.

2   Turner, J. C. (2005). Explaining the nature of power: A three-process theory. *European Journal of Social Psychology, 35,* 1–22.

3   Katz, N.H., Sosa, K.J., & Harriott, S.A. (2015). *Conflict management: Overt and covert dynamics. (pps. 38–42).* Unpublished manuscript, Department of Conflict and Analysis and Resolution, Nova Southeastern University, Fort Lauderdale, FL.

4   Ibid.

5   Ibid

6   Ibid

7   Ibid, 21

8   Johnson, L. K. (2011). *Keeping women silent: A study of female leadership in faith-based institutions* (Doctoral dissertation). Available from ProQuest Dissertations & Theses Global. (UMI No. 883589308)

9   Chang, P. M. Y. (1997). Female clergy in the contemporary protestant church: A current assessment. *Journal for the Scientific Study of Religion, 36(4),* 565-573.

10 Rose, S. D. (1987). The negotiation of gender in a charismatic community. *Sociological Analysis, 48 (3),* 245–58.

Chapter 7

1   Bridges, W. (2003). *Managing transitions: Making the most of change* (2nd ed). Cambridge, MA: Da Capo Press. Wildflower, L., & Brennan, D. (2011). *The handbook of knowledge-based coaching: from theory to practice.* San Francisco, CA: Jossey-Bass.

2   Kegan, R., & Lahey, L. (2001). *How we talk can change the way we work: Seven languages for transformation.* San Francisco, CA: Jossey-Bass.

3   William Bridges (2003), as outlined by Robert Kegan and Lisa Lahey (as cited in Wildflower & Brennan, 2011).

4   Prochaska, J. O., DiClemente, C. C., & Norcross, J. C. (2002). *Changing for good: A revolutionary six-stage program for overcoming bad habits and moving your life positively forward.* New York: Quill.

5   Keltner, J. W. (1994). *The management of struggle: Elements of dispute resolution through negotiation, mediation, and arbitration.* Cresskill, NJ: Hampton Press.

6   Bolman, L. G., & Deal, T. E. (2013). *Reframing organizations: Artistry, choice, & leadership* (5th ed). (p. 17). San Francisco, CA: Jossey-Bass.

Chapter 8

1   Senge, P., Roberts, C., Ross, R., & Smith, B. (1994). *The fifth discipline fieldbook.* New York: Doubleday.

2   Halevy, N., Cohen, T.R., Chou, E. Y., Katz, J. J., & Panter, A. T. (2013, October 21). Mental models at work: Cognitive causes and consequences of conflict in organizations. *SAGE Journals.* doi. org/10.1177/0146167213506468

Chapter 9

1   Cunningham, L. & Hamilton, D. J. (2000). Why not women? (p. 67–68). Seattle, WA: Youth With A Mission

2   Pastoral Care Inc. (2018). Statistics for Ministry. Retrieved from https://www.pastoralcareinc.com/statistics/

Chapter 10

1   Freire, P. (1968/1970). *Pedagogy of the oppressed 30th anniversary edition* (Translated by Myra Bergman Ramos). New York, NY: Bloomsbury.

2   Ibid, 55.

3   Freire, P. (1968/1970). *Pedagogy of the oppressed 30th anniversary edition* (Translated by Myra Bergman Ramos). New York: Bloomsbury.

4   Ibid, 48.

5   Ibid.

6   Ridgeway, C. (2009). Framed before we know it: How gender shapes social relations. *Gender & Society - Gender Soc.* 23, 145–60. doi: 10.1177/0891243208330313

7   Freire, P. (1968/1970). *Pedagogy of the oppressed 30th anniversary edition* (Translated by Myra Bergman Ramos). New York: Bloomsbury.

Chapter 11

1   Nason-Clark, N. (1987). Were women changing the image of ministry? A comparison of British and American realities. *Review of Religious Research,* 28(4), 330–40.

2   Trimm, C. (2019, September 19). The Essence, Your Divine Nature. Retrieved from https://www.youtube.com/watch?v=cZMmllvEWVY

3   Dewolf, M. (2017, March 1). *12 Stats About Working Women.* U.S. Department of Labor Blog. Retrieved from https://blog.dol.gov/2017/03/01/12-stats-about-working-women

4   Davis, N. L. (2019). *Women in ministry: How conflicts between God's purpose and church doctrine impact the efficacy of female church leaders* (Doctoral dissertation). Available from ProQuest Dissertations & Theses Global; Pro Quest Academic. (UMI No. 22584879)

Empower to Engage

1   Senge, P., Roberts, C., Ross, R., & Smith, B. (1994). *The fifth discipline fieldbook.* (p.3). New York: Doubleday.

CPSIA information can be obtained
at www.ICGtesting.com
Printed in the USA
BVHW031718051220
594963BV00002B/18